EARLY REVIEWS OF

The Board Member's Guide to Risk

"This is a great resource for board members, prospective board members, and organizations looking to add board members and structure to their boards. The writing is entertaining and clear and includes a brilliant distillation of your company's risk down to one key element that I will leave for readers to discover."
— Art Monaghan, Co-Founder, Granite Equity Partners

"This book is excellent. It's exactly the right length, tone, and, content. To cover a subject as broad as risk in such a succinct manner is testimony to the author's deep understanding of both the subject of risk and the role of corporate governance. While reading the book, it triggered my thinking on how the Boards on which I serve should be considering risk in a post-COVID virus environment. Building resilience, through Empowerment, Speed, and Trust was the biggest takeaway for me from the book. I look forward to sharing copies with my fellow Directors."
— Carol Gray, Board Member, IFM Investors; Board of Governors, Trent University; Board Member, Amex Bank of Canada

"The re-framing of risk in this book is really useful. Entire boards should read the book concurrently — so all are working from the same paradigm (or experience the same paradigm shift)."
— Sarah Oquist, Chair of the Board of Directors, Woodlands National Bank; Board Member, Walker Arts Center; Adjunct Faculty Member, Mitchell Hamline School of Law

"This book is exceptionally well-crafted and genuinely insightful. I believe it will become the "go-to" guidebook about risk for board members."
— Bartley J. Madden, Author, *Value Creation Principles*

"Reading this book was like drinking a fine bottle of wine. I finished it in one sitting! And yes, the book is like a good travel guide — it informs you of what you shouldn't miss on your risk-taking journey."
— David X Martin, Cyber Risk Management Expert; Special Counselor, Center for Financial Stability; former Chief Risk Officer, Alliance Bernstein; former Chairman and Chief Executive Officer, Knightsbridge Capital; Adjunct Professor, NYU Stern School of Business; and Author, *The Nature of Risk* and *Risk and the Smart Investor*

"Board members should read this book if they care even the tiniest little bit about how well they are doing at asking the right questions, making good decisions, and offering appropriate strategic guidance to their organizations when it comes to risk. David writes clearly, shares important insights, recounts anecdotes that bring these issues to life, and offers practical suggestions to use in the real world."
— Michele Wucker, Author, *The Gray Rhino*

"An excellent overview of how board members can improve their governance of the organization's risk-taking. The book is written in an engaging style with lots of useful examples and anecdotes. It provides several practical governance models to help guide decision-making and also has many helpful references for more in-depth research. It's a must read for board members looking to strengthen their organization's strategic decision making!"
— Jean Hinrichs, former Chief Risk Officer, Barclays Global Investors, and former Lecturer, Haas School of Business, UC Berkeley

"Books about risk normally make me feel like I'm drowning in an endless litany of risks, each one of which can pull me under. This book, by contrast, throws a lifeline. Several, in fact. It's written specifically to help board members, not to scare them into buying consultancy services. It's relevant, useful and practical."
— Jon Lukomnik, Managing Partner, Sinclair Capital; Co-Author, *What They Do with Your Money* and *The New Capitalists*

"This book does what it sets out to do — provide boards and individual board members with a framework for strengthening governance of their organization's risk taking and for pursuing their strategic goals successfully. The layout of the book holds together well, and chapters logically build on each other. The final chapter is particularly strong in summarizing, synthesizing, and suggesting future courses of action. It's a great resource."
— Sarah Forster, non-profit board member and Director of Milestone Reunions, Carleton College

"It is already on my must read list."
— David Finnie, co-Author, *Strategy, Risk, and Governance*; Board Member and Chair, Governance Committee, The Charles H. Best Diabetes Centre; former Chief Risk Officer, Central 1 Credit Union; and former Managing Director, the Global Risk Institute

"This is well-written, concise, fresh, and engaging. The two key refrains — risk is necessary, trust is essential — left me thinking about those two themes in relation to church and college settings where I spent my career. It seems to me, they are just as applicable there as in the world of business. The principles outlined in this book are timeless. The book is also timely. I hope it gets read widely and is adopted broadly. Well done!"
— W. Bruce Benson, Host of the *Sing for Joy* radio program and retired Senior Pastor, St. Olaf College

"There are many books on risk in general and on specific applications and subjects of risk management. Good and not so. If you're in a Board but for some reason you are not familiar with the concept the book is the right choice! It is likely you will not find [as] good [a] summary [as] David gave specifically for the board members."
— Mikhail Fedorov, "Risk Manager of the Year" in 2018 by Russian Risk Management Society

THE Board Member's Guide to Risk

David R. Koenig

(b)right governance
PUBLICATIONS

Copyright © 2020 by David R. Koenig. All rights reserved.

First edition, published by (b)right governance publications, Northfield, Minnesota.

No part of this publication may be reproduced, stored in a retrieval system, or transmitted in any form or by any means, electronic, mechanical, photocopying, recording, scanning, or otherwise, except as permitted under Section 107 or 108 of the 1976 United States Copyright Act, without either the prior written permission of the Publisher, or authorization through payment of the appropriate per-copy fee to the Copyright Clearance Center, Inc., 222 Rosewood Drive, Danvers, MA 01923, (978) 750-8400, fax (978) 646-8600, or online at *www.copyright.com*. Requests to the Publisher for permission should be addressed to (b)right governance publications, P.O. Box 52, Northfield, MN USA 55057.

Limit of Liability/Disclaimer of Warranty: While the publisher and author have used their best efforts in preparing this book, they make no representations or warranties with respect to the accuracy or completeness of the contents of this book and specifically disclaim any implied warranties of merchantability or fitness for a particular purpose. No warranty may be created or extended by sales representatives or written sales materials. The advice and strategies contained herein may not be suitable for your situation. You should consult with a professional where appropriate. Neither the publisher nor the author shall be liable for any loss of profit or any other commercial damages, including but not limited to special, incidental, consequential, or other damages.

For more information about this title or the author, please visit *www.davidrkoenig.com*.

Cover and book design by Holmes Design, Inc., Northfield, Minnesota.

Publisher's Cataloging-in-Publication Data:

Names: Koenig, David R., author
Title: The board member's guide to risk / David R. Koenig
Description: First edition. | Northfield, MN: (b)right governance publications, 2020
Identifiers: 9780578674810 (hardcover); 9798629628125 (paperback)
Subjects: Governance. | Economics — Value. | Boards of Directors. |
    Organizational effectiveness.
BISAC:
    BUS104000 BUSINESS & ECONOMICS / Corporate Governance
    BUS071000 BUSINESS & ECONOMICS / Leadership
    BUS042000 BUSINESS & ECONOMICS / Management Science
Library of Congress Control Number: 2020907306

Printed in the United States of America

10 9 8 7 6 5 4 3 2 1

IN DEDICATION

This book is dedicated to all who have stepped forward in the COVID-19 pandemic to help, especially the very courageous medical professionals who have risked their lives to save others, and have shown us all how to be brave. My father was a family doctor who passed away last year. And so, I also dedicate this book to his memory. With his black bag in hand, he was the classic doctor who made house calls, delivered babies, performed surgeries, saw you and your whole family in his office, and always knew that being a doctor went well beyond practicing medicine. He cared for the entire person — body, mind, and spirit — even if he would never have used that expression. Thank you to those who continue to care for others in this way, no matter your profession.

ACKNOWLEDGMENTS

My sincerest thanks to Bruce Benson, Sarah Forster, Carol Gray, Darlene Halwas, Jean Hinrichs, Sylvia Koenig, Jon Lukomnik, Bartley Madden, David X Martin, Art Monaghan, Amedee Prouvost, and Kirk Trow for their thoughtful readings of the first draft of the book. They have no responsibility for what I have written, but their comments and insights have made the book better.

I also want to thank all members of the DCRO Risk Governance Councils for the time they have given to share their best practices with the public. They are a knowledgeable and generous group of professionals, and I draw upon their wisdom.

I thank Barbara Cave Henricks and Marie-Josée Privyk for suggesting additional material to include in the book. Even if such suggestions seem minor, sometimes they are the perfect addition!

Many thanks to copy editors Helena Bachman and Don Bratland for their work. Don comes to his copy-editing through immense experience, giving him eyes that see things I cannot. Helena tries very hard to put my sentences on their best behavior.

Finally, I also want to thank Don Bratland and Holmes Design for the book layout, typography, and cover designs. Don and his wife are award-winning professionals for good reason. I am the beneficiary of both their talent and their friendship. If you find the book to be pleasing to look at, then you have benefited as well!

CONTENTS

Introduction   vii

Chapter 1 | The Meaning of Risk   1

Risk as loss   1
Risk as uncertainty   2
Risk as a return hurdle   3
Risk as an expense   4
Risk as a commodity   6
Risk and trust   7

Chapter 2 | The Effect of Risk on Decision-Making   11

The emotions of fear   11
Groupthink and acting under perceived threat   14
Groupthink and the "absence" of risk   14
Board composition and negating groupthink   15

Chapter 3 | Typologies of Risk Your Organization May Encounter   17

Financial Risk   17
Operational Risk   19
Technological Risk   20
Innovation Risk   21
Reputation Risk   22
Regulatory and Legal Risk   23
Misinformation Risk   24
Risk and trust   24
"Gray Rhinos" and "Black Swans"   25

Chapter 4 | Drivers of Your Success and the Threats to those Drivers — 27

Principal Component Analysis for boards — 27
Prioritizing drivers and threats — 31
Beginning to build resilience — 32
The financial benefit of resilience — 33
Validating corporate resilience — 35

Chapter 5 | Taking Risk Confidently — 37

Confidence — 37
Board reporting — 38
Real Options and choice — 39
Rampant incrementalism — 40
The value of distributed authority — 40
The value of risk as a line-item expense — 41

Chapter 6 | Corporate Risk Infrastructure — 43

Board committees — 43
Corporate risk committees — 45
The Chief Risk Officer — 46
Risk Silos — 47
Escalation channels and policies — 48
Trust-building: are your risk managers seen as value creators? — 49
Education — 49
An ethical culture — 50
Agility — 51

Chapter 7 | Board Processes Around Risk and Risk-Taking — 53

The Board Risk Committee — 54
Compensation Committees and risk — 56
Cyber risk governance — 58
Finding Qualified Risk Directors — 59

Chapter 8 | A Process of Continuous Innovation: Avoiding the "Fade" — **63**

The concept of "fade" — 63
The surprising mathematics of cities — 66
Knowledge-building proficiency — 67
A portfolio mindset — 68

Chapter 9 | Ongoing Conversations and the Feedback Loop: Always Getting Better — **71**

Our organization's social network — 72
Engaging your social network — 75
Stakeholder boards — 75
Executive sessions with employees — 76
Identification of Commons — 77
Successful Commons governance — 79
Trust and positive amplification — 80

Chapter 10 | The Next Steps to Take with Your Board Colleagues — **81**

Identifying key stakeholders — 84
Addressing Environmental, Social, and Governance concerns — 84
Gap identification — 86
Learn from others who planned to be resilient — 87
Engage exemplary board members — 89
Embrace diversity of opinion — 91
Bring humility and recognize our broad opportunity — 91
What's next? — 92

Appendix | The Meaning and Importance of a Positive Skew — **95**

INTRODUCTION

Businesses exist to take risk. Full stop.

In fact, all human organizations exist to take risk. Anytime we come together to try to serve some purpose or achieve some goal, we have assumed risk. If we didn't, we'd never advance beyond the status quo. In fact, not taking risk is probably the single surest way to be doomed to failure in the long-term, as innovation, competition, and customer lethargy slowly eat away at any advantage we may enjoy today.

You've likely heard the expression that risk and opportunity are two sides of the same coin. I find that to be erroneous. When we think of risk as loss and opportunity as gain, *risk* takes on a negative tenor. When risk is viewed simply as a negative, it frames our decision-making process about it. It puts it in a place of avoidance and all sorts of human biases kick in when something has a negative framing to it. We know that if risk is always seen negatively, we will be making sub-optimal decisions about taking it. That's human nature and one of the reasons for this book.

Good businesses take risk confidently. When we govern our organizations, we must welcome risk-taking in ways that are responsible and smart. Our governance models will help us gain that confidence and this book should start you on that path if you are not already there.

This book is not about risk management. That's for the people in your organization to do. Rather, this book is about how to make boards and individual board members better at the governance of an organization's risk-taking — the pursuit of the strategic goals you and your executives have identified. It's designed to be practical, helpful, succinct, and effective.

This is not the last thing you'll read about these subjects, but it's a great first overview that can serve to establish a common language around risk-taking discussions at your board. That's why each of your board members should read this book — maybe even at the same time.

This book is also like a travel guidebook. It won't tell you everything there is to see in a specific museum, but it will let you know which museums you don't want to miss on your journey. At the end of this book, you'll be guided to an online resource designed to help you find more information about everything discussed herein. On that site you'll also find conversations with other directors, executives, and thought leaders exploring what works best for them in their fiduciary roles. And if you find that you'd like a much deeper dive into the concepts developed herein, there are several books referenced on that site, including my first, *Governance Reimagined: Organizational Design, Risk, and Value Creation,* which fully builds-out the networked and distributive governance model I advocate.

Importantly, this book is also about recovery. As I finish my writing, the COVID-19 pandemic is still growing in the United States, where I live, but may be nearing an initial inflection point globally. We are responding, but many aspects of our economic life — and the total economic life of some organizations — are frozen. Debate presently rages about the proper balance to take between health and economic concerns going forward. How you think about and treat risk at the board level will impact how quickly your organization will recover from this health crisis, which has rapidly become a social and economic crisis too.

To begin our trip towards better risk taking, we must come to a common understanding about the meaning of the word *risk*. In other words, if risk is not just about loss, how do we discuss it when so many only see it as a negative? How *should* it be framed?

What kinds of risk should boards be thinking about? How do we do this in a way that emphasizes its role in the better achievement of our goals?

What kind of corporate infrastructure should we have supporting the board and also deployed in our organization?

Finally, how does this view of risk and risk governance help us to always be getting better at serving those who look to us for things they need or want? If you serve on the board of a nonprofit charity that provides human services, this is especially important for you now as demand for the vital work you do is likely surging and the resources to fund those demands may be in decline.

Board members naturally think about the future value of the organizations they serve — something that others will actually determine. That value can go up, down, or possibly stay the same. Risk is a way of describing a distribution of possible changes in that value, resulting from whatever risk-taking your organization chooses to do. Not every board member, however, is naturally aware of how critical external perceptions are in determining that future value. So, that's something we're going to discuss throughout the book.

The outcomes of risk-taking activities at our organizations are not like coin tosses — something equally likely to be better than worse. Rather, our job as governors of our risk-taking organizations is to create an environment that skews the bias of those outcomes towards a much greater likelihood of gain in value over loss.

That's why this book has been written for you — to read it, share it, and use it as you govern. Our goal is to give your organization's likely future value a *positive skew*.[1] And that's a valuable pursuit, no matter what you do.

---

1 *Skew* is a statistical term that describes one way in which a distribution of observations or predictions is different from a random set of data that has a normal or bell-curve distribution — whether there is a positive or negative asymmetry to the "bell." If that term is not familiar to you, there is a helpful illustration of it and its importance to your organization in the Appendix.

CHAPTER 1

The Meaning of Risk

Before our boards can have the most effective conversations about risk, it's important that board members have a common understanding of what risk means. If you surveyed the group today, before reading this book, it's highly likely that most would describe risk as the potential for loss or uncertainty about the future. Both are partially correct, but the missing parts of those definitions keep you from realizing the full potential of risk-taking at your organization.

In this chapter, we'll first address those two meanings of the word *risk* — loss and uncertainty. That's the easy part because they are so common. After that discussion we'll try to re-frame risk in several different ways. Our goal is to make it so that risk can be talked about in the same manner as you'd discuss capital expenditures, marketing strategies, performance, etc. We do this by reforming our mindset so that risk is about our future value — value that goes up and down from today, but not with equal likelihood.

It's value that we are trying to create in our endeavors, and we must take risk to do that.

Risk as loss

So, let's begin with risk viewed primarily as being about loss. Walking across a tightrope stretched between two buildings is risky because you might fall and lose your life. Crossing the street with your eyes closed is risky as well. Drinking smelly water is risky too. Why does it not smell like regular, safe water?

In short, you probably wouldn't do any of the three things above, because the fear of damage to your health has temporarily frozen you from action or your action taken is one of avoidance. Fear activates the fight-or-flight response and shuts down our rational and reasoning function. That part of the brain is slower to respond. If a real danger is charging at us, we don't want to be slowed down by anything!

We'll learn more about this in the next chapter, because sometimes shutting down reason and just reacting is okay. But in most cases, the negative framing of any choice — for example, "we could lose $3 million if we do this" — will change (in an unhelpful way) the decision that the firm ultimately makes. This bias has been demonstrated repeatedly by Nobel Prize-winning behavioral economists and psychologists with dramatic impact. We'll talk about how to fight this bias throughout the book.

When boards are considering long-term strategy, which involves the commitment of all forms of firm capital for extended periods of time, we want to be as clear-headed as possible. We don't want our known biases to cause us to be more likely to make an error in judgment.

Since you, me, and everyone alive today are evolutionary contemporaries, this physiological reaction isn't going to change during our lifetimes. So, we need to address it anywhere that humans impact our future value, including in our board rooms. No one gave fear the right to vote on plans.

Risk as uncertainty

We progress slightly from the impact of negative framing when we begin to associate risk with uncertainty. Uncertainty about the future value of something includes both increases and decreases in value. After making this association, we can begin to take risks without the full impact of negative framing affecting our decision-making. However, this conceptualization still doesn't give us any methods for being rational about risk. In fact, behavioral studies have shown that if there is a perceived potential for large loss as part of this uncertainty, we may require our perceived potential for gain to be two-and-a-half to three times the possible loss. That will eliminate several ventures that cumulatively could provide substantial returns and value-generation for our organizations, especially in a well-diversified portfolio of activities.

Risk as a return hurdle

When our emotions tell us to require double or triple the gains that we perceive as the potential for loss, our brains have determined a return hurdle that provides us with comfort. It may not be a rational hurdle, but it is a level only above which we will decide to act. An example of calculating hurdles in risk follows.

Consider a situation in which you find yourself walking down a hallway. You come upon a very dark room with a man standing just outside. He beckons and you cautiously approach. "I'll give you a thousand dollars if you go into this room, touch the wall on the other side, and then come back out," he offers. You have no idea what is in there and, in fact, just after this offer is made, some strange noises are heard emanating from the room.

Your assessment of this offer will be based on many things, including your personal biases and whether you have any level of trust in this person. But who wouldn't like $1,000?

In order to derive that value, though, you first have to ensure your survival. Those noises were not normal, and the room is pitch-black. How can you prepare yourself, so that you are more likely to achieve your goal?

Good news: Because you are an engaging person, you also have a network of resources on which you may call. You could buy a top-end flashlight for $100. With this light and for a fixed cost you can illuminate part of the room, reducing some of the downside potential. Maybe you'll be able see the source of the noises or any other potential dangers that lurk inside. However, even with this light, you cannot see everything in the room at once, so it may not be enough to entice you to take up the offer.

You recall that your neighborhood rental company has a searchlight of impressive strength. With it, you could illuminate almost the entire room, except for the area on either side and above the entryway. The cost to rent this searchlight is $400. Are you ready to enter and possibly net $600 for your mission?

Finally, a good friend comes along and says, "I'll go in for you if you pay me $800 up front." Does the fact that someone else will take the physical risks prompt you to take up the offer of the dark room's host? After all, if your friend makes it back, you figure you'll still be ahead $200. It's a far cry from $1,000, but at least your safety is no longer a concern.

In the end, what you're facing is a business decision, which is also a risk management decision.

In this example, the man and his dark room represent risk. He offers both upside and downside potential. The flashlight and searchlight are forms of risk management — things that illuminate the darkness and help you make a better (risk-adjusted) decision. Your friend-for-hire represents a concept called risk transfer, where, for a price, someone else will agree to assume the potentially life-threatening exposure you face.

Your ultimate decision is based on whether your expected return is sufficiently greater than your cost of pursuing the risk, especially in comparison to other opportunities.

In real life, we're beckoned into rooms of varying "darkness" with great frequency, especially as board members considering long-term strategic plans. The hurdles our company needs to pass in order to take risks will change, depending on how much light our infrastructure and processes shine on the current and future value of our effort.

Risk as an expense

In a way, hurdles cause us to put more thought into our choices and to set a standard for what we must expect on the positive side of risk-taking before we move forward. They can have a similar impact as allocated expenses. You and your colleagues may be more comfortable with this framing. Expenses? We can manage those! Are times tough? Manage expenses more carefully. How much does that new piece of equipment cost? We can afford that. It's in our budget.

Expenses are concrete. They may be variable, but they appear on our income statements and are part of the overall profit/loss or surplus/shortfall equation. We are comfortable with expenses because in our successful careers — those that earned us the invitation to be on this board — we manage them well and, likely, have done so for decades.

In our story above, we found out the cost of risk when we asked someone else to take the risk for us. We had the choice to pay $800 to possibly collect $1,000. In real life, we don't transfer most risks, we assume them among the portfolio of activities in which we engage. So, what is the respective cost of each venture we undertake? How can we view risk as a cost if we keep it in-house?

Our goal with this approach is to turn risk into a line-item expense. Chris Matten, who served as the group financial controller of Swiss Bank Corporation and was the Managing Director (Corporate Stewardship) of Temasek Holdings, remarked at a conference where he and I shared the stage that risk is the single largest item not appearing on an income statement. He was then and is still correct! Sadly, he made that comment back in 2003.

Our understanding of risk has progressed dramatically since that time, especially in terms of how we might turn it into a line item expense. We have more transparency, better markets, better technology, and a greater understanding of how much capital an organization needs to pursue its goals, collectively, or even on a project by project basis. This increased capability gives us the opportunity to more accurately assign costs for the risk-taking associated with our activities. If you are making a decision about a project and you are failing to incorporate all material costs, it is quite difficult to be making that decision well. That was Matten's complaint about poor accounting for risk.

Most things we deploy to pursue our goals have an expense associated with them. Are we keeping our payroll below 62% of revenue? What's our ongoing R&D expense? How much fixed infrastructure are we buying and what percentage of our revenue goes to debt service?

All these things are forms of capital — human, physical, and financial. These forms of capital have a cost. All organizations, therefore, have a total cost of capital. Note, this is not strictly the finance textbook cost of capital. But that's generally what we're getting at.

In all the cases above, we've had to find out what price we need to pay to get someone else to provide us with their capital. It might be their time and talent — their intellectual capital — or it might be bricks and mortar, or specialized equipment — that is, physical capital. Ultimately, all these require some form of financing, whether from current revenues, friends and family, credit cards, donors, bank loans, or through actively issuing debt or equity into the global financial markets.

Financing like this has a price ... and a limit. In fact, the closer you get to the limit set by external providers, the higher the price will become. We want to manage costs and make sure our organization is effectively incorporating the cost of risk-taking as an input to our pursuit of goals.

Risk as a commodity

Since all capital can be viewed as a commodity of some scarcity, the ability to acquire capital is not guaranteed. Have you asked HR what it was like to recruit in a world where the unemployment rate was 3%? Or, if your supply chains were interrupted, did you discover a change in the cost of that capital?

If risk capital is a commodity with an associated, but variable cost, we should make sure every time we spend money on risk-taking that it's likely to return more for us than it costs. If this is not the case, we shouldn't buy it. As a commodity, risk capital's availability is determined by the perceptions that others have of us. What is their upside in dealing with our organization compared to the downside, or relative to the cost of their capital? Do they have better options than working with us?

Like most commodities, risk capital is scarce. Therefore, when we shift our discussions about it to be in the frame of acquiring a good that has a price, it helps to keep it in a context familiar to most who have ascended to the place of serving as a director. It's also helpful to recognize the precious nature of risk capital as an input. It begins to solve Chris Matten's complaint and it makes us better at what we do.

The ability to take risk is not assured. As with other commodities, sometimes there are droughts that affect supply. With risk capital, though, sometimes those droughts are self-inflicted and avoidable.

Risk and trust

Now we get to the most important re-conceptualization of risk. Risk-taking is about its impact on trust. Trust is helpfully viewed as both "acceptable uncertainty" and, in relation to doing business with us, "a person's willingness to accept (and/or increase) their vulnerability."[1] Both are emotionally-driven assessments. So, when we govern risk well, the impact on trust will be positive, and we'll take away fear as one of the emotions that affects the degree to which others trust us and what they will charge us for their capital.

In my work to evaluate the link between good risk governance

---

1 Alex Todd, former Founding Principal of consultancy Trust Enablement Inc, shared these definitions with me during an insightful conversation about trust.

and value creation, I developed public company Trust Ratings. It was no surprise (at least to me) that the companies which garnered the highest levels of trust in comparison to those with the lowest trust, realized great benefit from their earned status. Over the twelve months following year-end 2017, companies so-ranked (high trust vs. low trust):

1. Had an effective weighted average cost of capital that was more than 30 basis points lower.
2. Experienced stock price volatility that was more than 30% lower.
3. Generated median "Economic Profit" of 11.4% versus -2.9%.[2]

In other words, trustworthy companies had higher performance and reduced uncertainty about that performance. This kind of result is found in other years as well. As a result, being trustworthy lowers the cost of ALL forms of capital. Hence trust, like risk capital, is a precious commodity.

Our discussion of risk is ultimately about what our organization does to build trust between us and all entities that provide us with capital — employees, customers, donors, suppliers, investors, creditors, retirees, etc.

Trust is something that makes all transactions easier and less expensive. Pursuing greater trust in this positive framing provides us with the mindset to take risk well. We seek to increase the valuable trust others have in us to deliver on their expectations. Progressing through the concept of risk capital as a scarce commodity, managing it as a line item cost, and ultimately tying it to the overall trust in your organization are the first steps toward improving your board's discussion of risk and risk-taking.

In sum, when we think and talk about risk, we're going to

---

2 Data is from year-end 2017 and is calculated using publicly available data through year-end 2018.

do so with these four things in mind:

1. The strategic decisions we make, and the execution of our corporate plans will increase or decrease the value of our organization by some unknown amount. We must take risk or that amount will ultimately, and with certainty, be negative.

2. The ability to take risk — our risk-taking capacity or risk capital — is a commodity that we compete to acquire. It can be drawn to us or it can run from us.

3. Since risk capital is a commodity, it has a variable price. Our organization must pay the price and should be thinking of that price as a line item cost like any other expense.

4. How much people trust our organization to meet their expectations is the main driver of this cost relative to our competitors. Higher trust will lead to lower costs and increased value.

CHAPTER 2

The Effect of Risk on Decision-Making

As alluded to in the first chapter, we want to turn risk into something we see as normal and recognizable. Ideally, we want it to be manageable by our people. As part of that process, we must understand how risk as loss, or more appropriately, risk as a threat, interferes with our rational and strategic thinking, as well as that of those who provide us with the risk-taking capacity.

The emotions of fear

Social psychologists have done remarkable research on the human behavior towards physical risks and any risks that threaten us in a material way. The 2008 subprime crisis and the ensuing Great Recession are a classic case study of how a loss of hundreds of millions of dollars in one sector was amplified many times over, ultimately causing trillions of dollars in losses around the world and across sectors that were completely unrelated to the original loss. This distortion of risk is called a social amplification, and it's a well-researched and understood phenomenon.

There are two factors that drive people to an emotional overreaction to an event they didn't expect. First, they wonder if it threatens them, personally. Could they die? Will they lose a lot of money? Will someone they love be greatly harmed? Or even, will their reputation be damaged through association with it?

Second, they wonder if anyone truly understands the problem that has emerged. Does it seem that experts in the subject are in charge? Have they been credible in the past? Do we continue to trust them now?

For a social amplification to occur, there needs to be both a high level of threat and a perceived lack of understanding, especially by experts, regarding the emerging issue. This was surely the case during the subprime crisis and was the initial response to the COVID-19 pandemic of 2020. Figure 2.1 shows some familiar negative risks and their position on this grid.

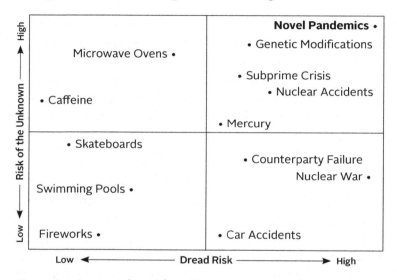

Figure 2.1. Source: Adapted from Slovic, Paul & Weber, Elke, *Perception of Risk Posed by Extreme Events*, prepared for discussion at "Risk Management Strategies in an Uncertain World," April 12–13, 2002.

To a lesser degree, amplification through fear and a lack of understanding can be realized in response to any service or product that your organization offers. We hope nothing you do endangers your customers and other stakeholders — those who depend on you as they plan forward. They trust you, to some degree, and if you lose that trust, or create a fear in them that you don't know what you are doing, that you are not reliable, or that your organization might go away, you can see a social amplification of abandonment of your products or services. This is another reason why thinking about risk in the context of trust is so important.

We process these events using three emotional forms.[1] The first focuses on the way in which people subjectively convert numbers — for example, data on a "100-year flood" — into how the event will impact them personally. The second focuses on how membership in a group or being part of a culture impacts how you perceive risk. Some cultures believe that certain risks require attention, while others pay little or no notice to these same risks. This can include cultures specific to one organization. The third looks at people's emotional reactions to risky situations and how perception affects their judgment. This emotional process is driven by the two factors mentioned previously — that something dreadful could happen to them personally, and whether anyone, especially experts, understands the source of the risk and how to control it.

In short, when this part of our brain is triggered, we are not making long-term, thoughtful choices. We are reacting only to survive. You don't want that kind of reaction from anyone providing capital to your organization, and you don't want it in the boardroom either. The cost and availability of the financial capital provided to you depends upon your ability to avoid any negative social amplifications towards your company. The same is true of all forms of capital, including human capital, or even the freedom to act devoid of burdensome regulations.

Social amplification stops, or is never realized, if people trust that you know what you are doing or that you will not greatly hurt or even just disappoint them. As we'll discuss later, social amplifications can also be positive, and that's another important part of governing your organization to be more likely to increase in value.

---

1 Princeton University professor Elke Weber describes these as axiomatic, socio-cultural, and psychometric paradigms. See Weber, Elke, "Risk: Empirical Studies on Decision and Choice", in International Encyclopedia of the Social & Behavioral Sciences, Elsevier Science, Ltd., 2001.

In later chapters, we're going to talk about the things you need to be looking for in your organization to maintain this trust, especially in reaction to something you didn't expect. Ahead in this chapter, however, we'll visit the boardroom and talk about the impact of fear and its presence among your colleagues.

Groupthink and acting under perceived threat

Groupthink is a well-known phenomenon and you may already be familiar with this concept. If not, the term describes how a closely connected group of people will tend to validate each other in a manner that keeps information that is contradictory to the group narrative out of the discussion. It's corrosive in the long run, and sometimes it can be disastrous.

If a closely-knit group is perceived to be under attack, the bond will tighten. There is an American expression, "circling the wagons," that describes how pioneers would move their covered wagons into a circle to create a boundary protecting them from attack by other settlers or natives of the land into which they had ventured. This is a helpful visual representation of the mental process of groupthink when our organizations are under attack.

The board, in this case, is not asking, "why are we being attacked?" Rather, it's responding impulsively to avoid dying. When groupthink is present, a forward-looking understanding of the issue that drove the attack in the first place may never make it to the table for discussion. Therefore, you cannot discuss how to modify firm behavior to prevent it.

Groupthink and the "absence" of risk

But this behavior can emerge not only when we are under attack. In fact, when times are great, or have been great for an extended period, self-congratulatory groupthink may prevent the board from considering new ideas or concepts that run counter to the given narrative of glory. Think of this reflecting a high level of trust in yourselves and your, perhaps perceived-to-be-superior, talent and skills.

In the trading rooms of my early career, the admonition was often heard that "the gods first make proud those they would destroy." Inevitably, all organizations find that some issue emerges and wipes the sheen off the grins of self-satisfaction. When this happens the response within the board and the organization itself may be similar to the loss of trust in experts — the reaction experienced by those involved in social amplifications. Disappointment relative to expectations damages trust. Lower trust, in turn, increases the cost of capital. And, less trust within the boardroom may, again, prevent you from putting the long-term, strategic part of your brain to work when you most need it. This is especially true if you feel threatened by the situation or by people whom you no longer trust.

Board composition and negating groupthink

I once was interviewed for a board position at a listed company whose board members regularly took vacations together. When the chair tried to ascertain whether I could "fit in" and not ruin their fun, I was sure this board was not for me. As it happened, I had earlier asked other board members how they ensure the company is always innovating, and their blank faces revealed they didn't have a good answer to my question — leading me to believe I wouldn't be a good fit anyway. But aside from this, the main point of my anecdote is that the chair of this board was seeking groupthinkers, perhaps without even being aware of it. He simply favored people who were like him.

It often takes only one voice of dissent from *inside* a group to break groupthink. The word *inside* is italicized because it is critical. That same person, with the same credentials, would not have the same effect if they were not a board member. This is true even if the board hired them to come in as a consultant and advise them. It has to be an insider — a member of the group.

This is why diversity of background, experience, gender, perspective, etc. is so important to the success of boards in governing their organizations' pursuit of value creation. It's also why we need voices from the front lines of risk-taking to give us independent perspectives — something we discuss in more detail in the second half of the book. We're trying to ensure that even under stress, or in times of prosperity, your individual and collective brains are not subjected to the very real emotional phenomena around fear or groupthink as our board seeks to ensure that we have the processes and resources in place to tilt risk-taking in our favor.

In summary, our organizations can be negatively impacted by fear from the inside as well as the outside. Sometimes this negative impact is massive because social amplification makes our problems much, much bigger. It is important to understand that even if you conquer fear in the boardroom, you may not have done so among those upon whom you depend. You need to be very aware of what drives their perceptions. This knowledge gives you a form of empathy and makes you a better board member and governor of risk. Our organizations can likewise be negatively impacted by closed groups — like the board. Established and continued trust that we earn will alleviate the former challenge, while a diversity of opinion within our small group will address the latter. Both can be turned to the positive side as well. We pursue trust and diversity because they will increase the value of our organizations, not just to help us avoid loss.

CHAPTER 3

Typologies of Risk Your Organization May Encounter

I've learned through humorous experience that risk and governance are not always the most popular topics for discussion. Whenever I am asked about my work at a party, inevitably the person with whom I am speaking sees someone on the other side of the room to whom they "must say hello!" Before you similarly excuse yourself from this chapter, note that for us to successfully move forward it's necessary to have an awareness of the sources and typologies of negative risk events that can drive fear, and to understand better why we are being charged for the types of risk we take in positive pursuit of our goals.

So, in this chapter, we're going to get everyone on the same page with some of the most essential comprehension of these risks — again which are usually, for now, framed negatively. Familiarity does not breed contempt. It breeds familiarity and comfort. We do not fear that which we understand. So, take your medicine here and move on.

Financial Risk

It's common for management-board discussions of risk to be about *Financial Risk*. In fact, almost all gains and losses from our risk-taking activities eventually become financial metrics. Still, in the common vernacular, financial risk is generally considered to relate to gains and losses from the change in a market price of a financial instrument, commodity, or service, or the cost and availability of capital. This can clearly be seen in the price of a stock or bond in your personal portfolio but is also found in the price of borrowing money at your organization, foreign exchange rates that impact international costs and revenues, short-term cash needs, or funding costs for inventory, for example.

Often these are broken down into three distinct areas. *Market Risk* specifically addresses changes in exchange rates, interest rates, stock prices, carbon prices, commodity input prices, and other market-priced variables and their impact on firm value and profitability or surplus. For the most part, these are outside of managerial control. So, it is thought that little competitive advantage can be gained from them. However, these are also risks for which both simple and advanced hedging strategies exist.

Because these risks and the opportunities to manage them are at a more advanced stage, significant competitive advantage can be gained by understanding and managing market risks better than your competitors. I once ran risk management for a mortgage company that ranked 23rd in market share. When there was a significant disruption in the interest rate markets in 1994, our investment in technology and modeling of some very complex risks gave us an almost unrivaled understanding of the impact market conditions like that would have on our profitability. Because we understood our risks better, it allowed us to be more aggressive in our pricing than our competitors. We also had high trust levels between our risk group and customer-facing employees on whom our clients depended. Our customers already had high trust in them, and that trust was enhanced when they benefited from our management of the crisis. When I met several of our customers at a party the organization threw later that year, no one excused themselves to the other side of the room, which was a pleasant change.

Because of the pre-planning and investment in knowledge and technology at this company, we quickly moved from 23rd to 9th place in market share and were one of the only major mortgage lenders to be profitable that year. Many years later the mortgage company was sold for a profit of more than $700 million.[1]

Interestingly, pressure to sell the mortgage company came about because it had become too successful. Its growth had caused some rating agencies to worry about its size relative to the parent company — an insurer that needed to maintain a stellar credit rating. This was a better problem to have than a forced sale due to losses.

Credit Risk pertains to an organization's exposure to the failure of a counterparty to a transaction involving payments or a loan. It's a failure to fulfill an obligation — a breach of trust. As such, this is usually something discussed referencing the potential for loss in the event of default. Having a better understanding of your vulnerability to credit risk, though, can allow you to take risk more confidently through extending your exposures in this realm. There may be clients or suppliers whose credit profile you understand better than others.

Liquidity Risk is the loss of short-term financing to facilitate the daily transactions of the organization, or unexpected demands for funds that cannot be met in a timely fashion. Loss of access to this capital can come from events completely external to your organization. The extent to which you have built high levels of trust and loyalty from those who provide the financing to you will give your organization ongoing competitive advantage. You may realize lower funding costs in the short-term as well as long-term advantage through a reduction in the likelihood that a liquidity event will impact you more severely than others who offer substitutes for your products or services.

Operational Risk

Operational Risk is generally defined as the risk of loss resulting from inadequate or failed internal processes, people, and systems. It's often a catch-all for losses that occur due to human

---

[1] *Principal Sells Mortgage Unit to Citigroup*, Associated Press, May 2004.

or technological failures outside of what had been addressed through other risk analysis. These can include *Security Risk*, like employee safety, executive protection services, and barriers to access of a organization's physical infrastructure.

Other operational risks include *Supply Chain Risk*, which is exposure to other agents in your network upon whom you rely to supply goods or services that are part of your organizational process, or the delivery of your goods or services. Also, *Business Continuity Risk*, which is the disruption of your organization's ability to operate in its usual locations or use its normal technologies due to natural or other factors. *Third- and Fourth-Party Risk* is a challenging operational risk because it is your exposure to the subcontracting done by the subcontractors with whom you work. It is both your and their operational risk.

It's generally believed to be more difficult to attain any upside from operational risk. But when we discuss Gray Rhinos later in this chapter, and the value of resiliency later in the book, you'll see that there is actually significant value to be generated by understanding and preparing for these risks better than your competitors. How you respond to them matters greatly.

Technological Risk

Nearly all of us are familiar with *Cyber Risk*, ideally through its impact on others. In truth, the only difference between companies that have acknowledged intrusions to their data and digital infrastructure, and those that have not, is that the latter do not have the resources to identify the attacks and subsequent losses. It's likely those intrusions continue concurrent to your reading of this book. I can promise that the realization of cyber risk has happened to your organization as I assume you do valuable things.

Prime targets for those seeking such intrusions include data regarding your customers, employees, partners, and other members of your organization's social network. *Data Governance* and *Cyber Risk Governance* are terms often assigned to the managerial process in overseeing this certain vulnerability, although the latter has a counterpart at the board-level which we discuss later in the book.

Most often, cyber risk is the result of *Technology Risk*, which is the failure of a technological agent in a system or inadequacy of technology. Technology risk extends beyond cyber risk, though, into the systems you use to serve your customers, your processes around innovation, your physical plant and equipment, the infrastructure of your supply chain, and any other technology that is an integral part of your ongoing growth and service. It doesn't have to be digital to be a technology risk and this form of risk is not just about keeping people from seeing your firm's digital "Crown Jewels." Ask Research in Motion, the makers of the Blackberry, or Kodak if they experienced any technology risk. While their vulnerabilities and experience also reflect innovation risk (discussed next), both Kodak and Research in Motion are two high-profile, global examples of technology risk on the loss side of future value.

Innovation Risk

One of the most important sections in this book is the one where we talk about competitive fade, the surprising mathematics of cities, and knowledge-building. That discussion focuses on remedies for *Strategic Risk*, which is the misalignment of corporate goals with the needs of those to whom you are connected, or innovation external to the system that replaces or acts as a substitute for an organization's goods or services.

The story of Nokia's multiple reinventions of itself is a classic case of the upside of innovation risk, while, as I mentioned above, there are many, many lessons about the downside. Google/Alphabet, Amazon, and 3M are famous for their continuous innovation and experimentation. If your organization is not innovating, you are simply waiting to go away. This echoes the first guidance of this book, that being afraid to take risk is the surest way to fail.

You are taking the medicine in this chapter, in part, so that you are inoculated against that fear.

Reputation Risk

One of the most helpful ways to describe *Reputation Risk* is the future ability of an organization to persuade. This applies to every transaction in which the organization is involved. It may be customer acquisition, the acquisition of financial capital, the imposition, or not, of regulatory requirements, and the ability to deal with issues related to the people who help you define and reach your goals. The future value of your brand is subject to reputation risk.

But reputation risk has impact across all forms of capital acquisition. *Human Capital Risk* includes your ability to attract and retain top talent, your foresight in addressing changing social norms for which you may be accountable today or in distant years — do you have a handle on what is changing now, and your integration of human talent into your innovation processes? There is also some technology risk underlying reputation risk. LinkedIn is doing highly valuable work helping companies to know where they are losing or winning the talent game, and from whom they might poach talent. If you don't know what LinkedIn and the beneficiaries of its data are doing, your risk in this area is growing.

You might think it odd to include *Environmental Risk* — the potential impact of your organization's activities on the environment — in this section, unless you extend the definition similarly to the way in which changes in social norms can impact human capital risk. Changes in the environment in which we operate will affect our ability to pursue corporate values. Our environment is both the natural world in which we operate, live, and breathe, as well as the business climate in which our pursuits take place. Failure here significantly impacts our ability to influence, while success greatly enhances trust in us, our ability to look forward into the future, and the cost of all our transactions.

Regulatory and Legal Risk

I've often been asked why companies adopt risk governance or risk management programs. What I have found is that the source of a commitment to good risk governance comes from one of three sources. The value likely to be realized by these drivers is highest when the source is an educated board and management team that understands risk in the way in which it is described in this book. Risk governance and the active management of risk by employees becomes recognized as value-adding, and part of overall strategic and operational plans.

The second source has to do with bad experiences — either internally or through the witness of a close-competitor's travails. Wanting to avoid future damage to the organization from similar sources of exposure, firms adopt checks and balances to identify potential failures. This generally puts risk into the negative frame we so want to avoid.

But far and away, the least helpful reason for organizations to adopt practices around risk, is because they are told they must. The loss experiences described above may actuate *Regulatory Risk* — changes in or initiation of regulation by some government or industry group. There are few taxes on our work that are as easily identifiable as required compliance with regulations made in response to some loss, either internally, or at another firm like yours.

All the processes required to achieve our goals create *Legal Risk*, which is the failure to comply with existing regulations, errors in legal agreements, or litigious actions against an organization. It's really difficult to find upside from either legal risk or regulatory risk, except that an awareness of their downside can inform discussions about the importance of quality and the governance and management of all other risks that we choose to take. And, again, we must take risks to grow or even to survive.

Misinformation Risk

"Fake News" is a sadly relevant term in contemporary dialogue. Its use is intended to undermine the credibility of those seeking to hold political figures accountable for their actions. But the concept is believable because nefarious agents are indeed operating, sometimes on a global scale, to produce false information about people and organizations. This information may be a direct assault — using names — or, as is more often the case, an indirect attempt to undermine confidence. It concerns decision-making by leaders who may not know if they can trust the sources of information used in strategic planning or execution.

And what about partners in your pursuit of corporate goals, who may wonder if their previous assessments of your organization are inaccurate? Should they be worried? Has their trust in you been misplaced? This is *Misinformation Risk*.

Risk and trust

What's common among all the typologies of risk discussed above is that each is reflective of an erosion of, or potential enhancement of, trust. As mentioned at the start of the book, the impact of risk-taking on trust is the most important way for us to be discussing risk at the board level. A loss of trust negatively impacts our value, as every goal we pursue, or need we have, becomes more expensive when trust is damaged. The enhancement of trust, however, reduces the costs we incur and boosts the willingness of those who provide us capital to allow us to take on risk. That makes us substantially more valuable in the long-run.

Ultimately, the integration of all moving parts in the organization in a risk management framework is called *Enterprise Risk Management* or ERM. ERM, done properly, is focused on the maximization of our organization's future value based on our risk-taking capacity. Enterprise Risk Management builds trust both internally and externally.

"Gray Rhinos" and "Black Swans"

Finally, a discussion of risk typologies would be incomplete without the mention of Gray Rhinos and Black Swans. You likely are familiar with Nassim Taleb's integration of Black Swans to the common business vernacular. These are events that were believed to be highly unlikely, as they had never before been seen. If you believe that the world only has white swans, your world view has to change when you are introduced to black swans, which do exist. Sometimes that change can involve an emotional response, which usually impairs your ability to make thoughtful, long-term decisions. One of our goals in governing risk better is to moderate emotional reactions to Black Swans. Further, we want to have built-in the capacities in our organization to respond to such surprising events and, perhaps, even benefit from them.

You may not be as familiar, though, with Gray Rhinos. Michele Wucker is the author of *The Gray Rhino: How to Recognize and Act on the Obvious Dangers We Ignore*. It's a fascinating and well-written examination of why individuals and groups fail to act when they see high-probability, high-impact events heading right at them — the strategic equivalent of a charging Rhino. According to Wucker:

> "Gray rhinos are not random surprises, but occur after a series of warnings and visible evidence. The bursting of the housing bubble in 2008, the devastating aftermath of Hurricane Katrina and other natural disasters, the new digital technologies that upended the media world, the fall of the Soviet Union ... all were evident well in advance."[2]

Like our understanding of how fear causes us to shut down parts of our brain focused on the long-term perspectives, there

---

2 Michele Wucker's website for *The Gray Rhino*, www.wucker.com/writing/the-gray-rhino, last accessed April 25, 2020.

is significant evidence that we also fail to mitigate future events that are likely to cause great damage to us. It's a story of human psychology that, much like counteracting the harmful impact of framing risk in the negative, can be overcome by understanding it better.

Now, you have a common and hopefully better knowledge of the terms your employees may throw around when discussing risk. Was that so bad? Being familiar with the terms above and their potential impact on your organization, positive and negative, makes it easier for you and all your colleagues to have an educated discussion about risk.

Medicine taken; we are ready to move on.

CHAPTER 4

Drivers of Your Success and the Threats to those Drivers

First principles are the core of knowledge and understanding and can be used to reverse-engineer complicated problems. First principles are the building blocks of reason and rational thinking, of successful strategic planning, and of using our risk-taking capacity.

We begin with the first principles of our success in achieving goals because the moving parts ultimately intersect in complex ways that can amplify positively and negatively. They may be much harder to understand at that point and are certainly much harder to govern. We need to have a firm and relatively simple foundation from which to build our risk governance infrastructure.

We start with the end goal of success, then work backwards. We first ask, what is our purpose? Then we move to the drivers of success in living that purpose. And next we identify the key structural components of those drivers. These are the first principles of that which will determine our organization's future value.

Principal Component Analysis for boards

The recognition of directional movement in demand for our products caused by some other factor is derived by performing *Principal Component Analysis* or PCA. It's an elementary form of both risk management and asset/liability management that identifies first principles of our success. It's a form of SWOT (strengths, weakness, opportunities, and threats) analysis. We want to break down complicated problems into basic elements and then reassemble them from the ground up. It's one of the best ways to move from linear to non-linear results on the positive side of risk-taking.

An illustration might help to explain this. I once was asked by a board member of a mid-sized nonprofit that served families in need of food and support to help him with a quandary around their endowment's investment strategy. Having just come out of the Great Recession, their organization had faced unexpected strains from the need for their services. Absent an endowment from which they could draw reserves in high-demand times, their board decided to start one in anticipation of the next time a crisis emerged.

This nonprofit is highly regarded in the region that they serve. Hence, they achieved a relatively quick success in funding the endowment. Next came the discussion about investment of those assets. One board member, who was familiar with investment management but perhaps not as appreciative of investment risk, suggested equities as the dominant investment vehicle. He said that they offered the best long-term performance of asset classes available to the nonprofit. The director who contacted me said this didn't feel right to him, but he was not sure why.

Your initial sense might be that the cautious director simply feared equities to be too risky, especially given what had happened when the subprime crisis erupted. Perhaps he was afraid it could happen again. I explained to him that he was partially correct to have this concern. But the answer to why he should feel discomfort really was in understanding the drivers of their "business."

Lower unemployment generally means less demand for free food and clothing. Higher unemployment, on the other hand, increases the need for these services. When stock prices go up, unemployment tends to go down. And, when stock prices fall, unemployment rates grow and so does the need for social aid.

The assets suggested by his colleague were exactly "wrong-way." In other words, if the stock market crashed, so too would the value of their endowment, just as demand for the organization's services would increase. Such an event with stocks dominant in the portfolio would force the institution to begin external fundraising at a time when everyone else was experiencing a decline in their assets and might be fearing for their own situation. At that point, they would be less able to fund the nonprofit's needs.

On top of this, if times were good, the organization may have garnered a false sense of security that its large and growing endowment would be sufficient to meet any future needs. If that were the case, they might be less aggressive in regular fundraising or may even add costly services they believe they now could afford. They might even begin to groupthink in a manner driven by hubris over their very "wise" decision to invest in equities.

Over two weeks in March 2020, as the emerging pandemic forced social distancing and the closure of many service businesses, stock prices fell by more than 30%. Demand for the services of this nonprofit is skyrocketing in response to the economic distress.

I don't know what assets they ultimately decided to use in the endowment fund. I do know that the advice I shared with the cautious director was mocked by the "investment-savvy" board member. I hope that someone, perhaps an insider, ultimately broke that mindset.

I am not suggesting that managing the risk faced by this nonprofit would be easy. But the need to see resources grow when demand grows is basic asset/liability management. Implemented properly, this nonprofit would be far more valuable to its clients and would become even more highly respected by its supporters were it to structure itself according to these principles.

In another example of why this principal component analysis is so important for boards, we look at a case where a board could have established an environment of trust that would have greatly benefited their organization. Some organizations use income from their investments to fund general expenses. It's not a great plan, but it isn't uncommon. Around the same time that I had the discussion with the board member at the nonprofit mentioned above, the Chief Financial Officer of a large institution that relied on investment returns to fund operations asked me if I knew whether any of his competitors were engaging in asset/liability management like that which I recommended to him. His organization had likewise suffered an impairment to their ability to operate because of investment losses during the Great Recession. I told him that I did not, but pointed out that it was common practice in other industries. Every savings and loan association started to adopt this approach after many of them failed in the late 1980s, and several other types of institutions did as well when shown its value. These organizations all understood fundamental first principles about their companies.

Noting that none of his direct competitors was engaged in asset/liability management, he said, "then why would I?" And the conversation ended.

During any future prolonged stock market corrections or bear markets, his organization will be more likely to need holes in their budget to be fixed. If realized, that condition will break trust with employees and customers. Careful analysis of the principal components of their success might have steered him or his board differently.

Alas, being like everyone else is safe. Avoiding the consequences of standing out alone is a fear-driven response. This CFO wasn't totally irrational in this choice. But if his board had recognized this corporate vulnerability and given him permission to be an outlier, they'd have seen opportunity in the market sell-off of March 2020. Perhaps they could be taking advantage of opportunities to recruit talent that their competitors will likely be releasing in the coming months or to invest in new ideas those competitors can no longer afford.

Prioritizing drivers and threats

Upon completing a PCA-type analysis, it's common to take these principle drivers and threats and put them into an action matrix. The matrix has two axes — one being *probability* and the other *impact*. This is to say that one quadrant identifies low probability / low impact events, while the quadrant diagonal to it identifies high probability / high impact events — the Gray Rhinos (see Figure 4.1). This matrix was incorporated into the original COSO framework that many auditors use, as it can be very helpful to boards and executives.

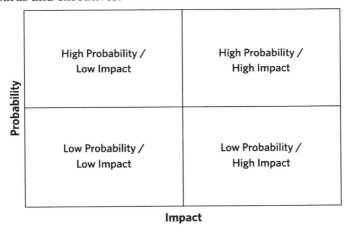

Figure 4.1 Typical Risk Assessment Grid

The matrix is helpful when it focuses our attention and actions on the most important places. One element of importance is that we can use it to identify where fear might be encroaching on our decision-making around certain elements, or where we are not taking action while Rhinos are charging right at us. Still, the matrix is missing one critical component, and that is an identification of the drivers that have the potential to lead to social amplification. These drivers need a separate prioritization by the board as they evaluate the ability of the organization to respond, which we discuss next in this chapter. If you don't do this, you create an unknown downside risk to your organization and are likely not realizing the full upside potential of some risks you can take.

Beginning to build resilience

For a moment, let's focus on *resilience* — our organization's ability to respond to emerging downside risks, especially those that are surprising us via amplification. There are three key components to establishing this resilience that come only *after* you have prioritized downside risks and identified those with the potential to amplify.

1. Empowerment — The distribution of authority to those who are closely placed to the origin of risks, especially customer-facing employees, is critical. If given this freedom and appropriate resources, they can mitigate emerging issues directly with customers or through escalation channels within the organization. Additionally, the organization should establish a form of rapid response, often called a *Problem Response Team*, at the very senior levels. At this point in the organizational structure, larger decisions can be made which might have significant consequences or benefits for the firm and which might also cut across multiple areas of responsibility simultaneously.

2. Speed — Rapidity of response is often essential. In the early days of the COVID-19 viral pandemic, the impact of days' or weeks' delay in responding to its discovery have been dramatic. Negative risks that are amplifying and are specific only to your organization often act just like viruses, spreading through the networks of those who are engaged with you. Your organization must be structured to address them quickly.

3. Trust — There it is again. Those whom you have empowered to act with speed must trust that their actions will

not be criticized or that they will suffer consequences if their actions turn out to have been sub-optimal. This is a guarantee that the board and senior executives must make. Further, those who are part of your organization's social network must trust that you are acting expediently, with knowledge, and with care for them.

We'll look at this topic more closely when we discuss board and organizational infrastructure and processes in Chapters 6 and 7.

The financial benefit of resilience

Remember the importance of assigning a cost to risk? We have a handy reference to help us understand just how valuable resilience can be when we look at credit ratings used by banks and debt issuers; let's tie them to line-item expenses. Credit ratings are usually expressed using grades like those received in school: a range of As, Bs, and Cs. From one agency, they range from AAA, which is almost non-existent because the risk of default on the credit is so small, down to C (a rating of D means the entity has defaulted). Figure 4.2 shows these relative expected default rates by letter grade.

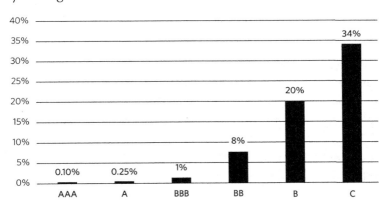

Figure 4.2 The probability of default by credit rating.
Source: European Commission

Banks are required to hold more (costly) capital for higher-risk credits to which they lend money. In other words, because it is more likely that a company with a BB rating will default than one with an AA rating, the banks are required to hold more capital against that loan. Capital as a line-item expense means all-else-equal; a loan to a BB-rated entity requires them to get more revenue from the borrower (charge the borrower a higher cost) in order to make the loan profitable. It has a higher hurdle to pass. See Figure 4.3 for an illustration of this.

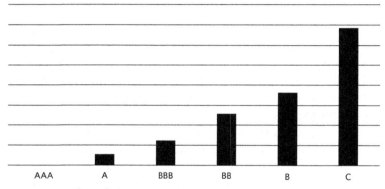

Figure 4.3 The relative increase in costs to borrow by credit rating.
Source: Federal Reserve Bank of New York

These ratings are driven by the trust that rating agencies have in a borrower's ability and willingness to pay back the loan. Risk management and risk governance, especially at organizations which use the approaches outlined in this book, will lead to an assessment by these rating agencies that suggests it is far less likely that company will realize losses that ultimately cause default. And, if these organizations have identified potential sources of negative amplification and built the processes to intercept them, they can receive even higher ratings. Higher ratings indicate higher trust. Higher trust means lower costs — that's a competitive advantage. It's a line-item savings that flows straight through to the bottom line of your performance.

But the financial benefit of resilience is not just limited to its impact on borrowing costs. In fact, any project, business unit, or venture has some probability of not meeting expectations or even incurring losses that exceed the capital allocated for it. To the extent that we engage systems that build resiliency in the organization, we reduce the risk of seeing losses of that magnitude because problems are intercepted before they can reach their full potential impact. That reduces the amount of capital needed, and much like a better credit rating reduces borrowing costs, the cost of capital to fund that risk-taking venture is reduced and the bottom line is improved.

Validating corporate resilience

How do you know if your organization is likely to be resilient? Let's first look at two methods for checking that are commonly used. *Stress Tests* and *Scenario Analysis* are important risk games to play at the board and executive level. Stress tests are when the risk experts in your organization create highly unlikely events that cause stresses on your exposures and drivers identified above. They may also extend to items you think are not related to your success, but which could become relevant under stressed conditions.

Scenario analysis, or table-top exercises, involve the dynamic assessment of specific threats. For example, if you have a factory along a riverfront, or a water-treatment plant in a similar location, what would happen if an upstream natural event caused flooding? What level of stress could potentially knock either of these out? Scenario Analysis is also valuable in helping to anticipate the impact of future events because the scenarios bound the realm of that possibility, making it easier to comprehend and process without fear of the unknown impacting our judgment.

Des Moines, Iowa learned one cost of unanticipated events after it lost its entire clean-water supply following record floods in 1993. In *The Gray Rhino*, author Michele Wucker talks about some Canadian provinces and cities that experienced similar disasters and made the necessary investments ahead of time. So, when the next flood came, they were ready.

A third approach is one that taps into external knowledge and experience. *External Risk Audits* are valuable as well, although I hesitate to equate them with games. Modern risk management has been practiced, now, for close to 35 years. That means that there is a growing number of former executives in risk management who have lived through all kinds of stresses, specific to industries, specific to political geographies, or broadly non-discriminatory in impact like market disruptions or pandemics. Many of these people can quickly tell a board if their infrastructure and processes look sufficient, given the complexity of their pursuits; they are probably even more valuable than external financial audits for anticipating the distribution of future financial performance.

One final note about understanding the first principles of our success relates to the strategic choices that we make. In their forthcoming book, *Strategy, Risk, and Governance*, James Darroch and David Finnie emphasize this idea of focusing on the principal component drivers of success by saying, "Your strategic goals and position create the risks that you need to manage." Their focus is on execution within the organization. At the board level, our focus is on understanding how and why to give our people permission to execute on the resiliency we need to enhance our competitive position, especially when those around us did not and are subsequently suffering the consequences. As you read the next three chapters, you'll be able to identify the parts that you may be missing in this pursuit.

CHAPTER 5

Taking Risk Confidently

This is where we want you and your board to get — to a place where talk of taking risk stimulates a rational and confident discussion about strategy, free of the emotional encumbrances of fear of loss. I hope you've been inoculated against fear of risk. You now know that such fear leads to worse decision-making on your part because your brain is hard-wired to respond to threats in such a way. And maybe you've committed yourself to learning more about each of the subjects mentioned so far. If so, even better!

The next three chapters are about how board governance can be designed to foster confident risk-taking by your enterprise. Later in the book we'll learn why such an action is necessary if you want to avoid becoming a "lesson-learned" case study for future MBAs. Before that, we'll talk about how to get to that point.

Confidence

Mark Twain is quoted as wryly observing that "ignorance and confidence can take a man a long way." An image of someone you know may have just popped into your mind! We are all subject to falsely believing that success implies skill. It almost always spawns confidence. But leaving outcomes to a combination of ignorance and confidence is not likely to have a positive future skew. Our goal in governance of risk is to think that if Twain were alive today, he would assign a far less dismissive attitude towards you and your board. We want you to have confidence, but that confidence will come from knowledge, along with planning about risk and the likelihood of our decisions increasing the value of the enterprise.

Board reporting

I once was shown a board committee report that contained approximately 250 pages of data. It was given to a board member as part of his Finance Committee assignment. He was incredulous regarding the expectation management had put upon him to know and understand these metrics. My sense was that management had at least one ulterior motive, and that was to shift liability one step higher in the organization. If you've been given the data, "you should have known." With validation of this suspicion, he pushed back on the contents of the report and, my understanding is, it later became far more succinct and actionable.

Data is important, but contextual analysis among an educated and diverse set of peers will be far more helpful. In Chapter 7, I reference several key documents that have been developed to guide your board committees, and ultimately the board, to a helpful and productive discussion about risk in the context of achieving goals. These documents were developed by a global collection of board members and C-level executives, whose responsibilities and experiences are in the governance of risk-taking. Risk considerations, under the guidance of this book and these documents, will be about trust-building, appropriate cost allocation, return hurdles, and building value — all associated with the word *risk*. Risk governance by the board will be about empowering your CEO to pursue strategic corporate objectives with the same mindset of confidence about risk-taking and within the behavioral parameters you think make the organization's success most likely. Once you implement these goals, board reporting will migrate to a mix of data, forward-looking strategy, evaluation of past performance, and risk, in its positive contexts.

Real options and choice

What you face with each strategic choice at the board level is something called a *Real Option*. A real option is the right or opportunity that you have to make some strategic allocation of your risk-taking capacity. You will have some limit to your ability to utilize the commodity called risk. It has an increasing price when you take too much or approach the limit of what others think you are capable of handling. These real options include choices about expansion, acquisition, closure or abandonment, delay or acceleration of an investment or commitment, and future performance hurdles that may trigger further investment or withdrawal from a project.

Real option valuation is helpful when dealing with another kind of risk animal, the White Elephant. White Elephants are physical infrastructure, products, or even business units whose cost of upkeep is not covered by the value they generate. Often these are items that have become institutionalized or have a long history which may, at one point, have included high value generation.

Real options are evaluated using inputs that include upfront investment costs, current valuation, the distribution of possible future valuations, how long this opportunity exists, borrowing costs, and likely cash flows in the future. Your borrowing costs are lower if trust in your organization is higher. The distribution of future valuations is skewed positively when you have good risk governance in place. Both lower borrowing costs and the positive skew make the real options presented to you more valuable — an example of the positive impact the right risk governance mindset and process can have.

Real options are not thumbs-up or thumbs-down decisions. They are necessarily presented as choices. And, as research has shown, if you consider projects in isolation, you may be as much as 30% more likely to make an error in your choice. But you cannot effectively evaluate real options unless you have a good risk governance structure in place.

Rampant incrementalism

As an officer of the Principal Financial Group, I first encountered the concept of rampant incrementalism. Insurance companies are staid, conservative places. Recall the story told earlier in the book about the increasing risk that a very successful mortgage company was perceived to be causing for its parent company, the insurer? That was the Principal Financial Group. I expected the Principal, as it is commonly called, to be afraid of risk and somewhat stuck in its ways. On the contrary, the firm, led by David Hurd at the time, was always innovating, always moving forward, just doing so in small steps. There was a culture of rampant experimentation and innovation that never started out too big. It was hugely successful.

Recall earlier when we discussed the idea that many people will require two to three times the expected gain if they perceive the possibility of large, destructive loss to be present. Rampant incrementalism kept the fear of large losses off the table. That meant that even marginally accretive innovations could see the light of day and the portfolio of those marginally accretive strategies provided great returns, even if some, or many, failed. This portfolio-of-small-risks approach allowed for a real financial mitigant to these losses, while the mindset, ex ante, provided a mitigant to the impact of fear on decision-making.

Firms have different tolerance for losses. But having processes in place that can limit the amplification or acceleration of losses to unanticipated levels is a key element in creating the positive skew to the future value of any organization. This is a direct impact from the resiliency-building discussed in the previous chapter.

The value of distributed authority

Also, as discussed in the previous chapter, empowerment of those closest to the origin of risks being taken is essential for speedy interruption of emerging issues. These same people play a key role in bringing innovative ideas back to the decision-makers. We're going to spend more time on this idea later in the book. But note that distribution of authority requires trust. Trust comes from better risk governance. Better risk governance yields a more positively skewed distribution of future valuations to what you do. Do you note a recurring theme here?

The value of risk as a line-item expense

No matter your dedication to implementing best practice risk governance, it is not reasonable to expect that all employees understand the concepts of risk, let alone risk capital allocation. But every employee is a risk manager, potentially. So, turning risk into an expense can make them much smarter about the cost of risk than trying to teach them to be knowledgeable as an MSc in Risk Management. We do this by developing an understanding of both the cost to the firm of acquiring the capital to take risk and the relative change in the firm's future costs that could come from this business unit's risk-taking, or even the capital required by one specific project.

We can begin with consideration of how each unit or project would be funded, and the cost of that funding, as a stand-alone. But that's not the board's job. Rather, the board should be ensuring that the infrastructure is in place to reasonably calculate the cost of risk. That will be part of our examination of board committee work and the internal corporate infrastructure around risk over the next two chapters.

We need both of these — best-in-class risk governance at the board level and best-in-class risk management running through the organization — to give us the confidence to take risk well. The value of this can be immense.

CHAPTER 6

Corporate Risk Infrastructure

As mentioned earlier, the engagement of external risk auditors — those having substantial, applied experience with enterprise risk systems — is highly valuable. They can help you to evaluate the existing infrastructure within your organization, such as data, technology, human capital, culture, etc. Their guidance can tell you if that infrastructure has any gaps that need to be addressed — gaps that may prevent you from making fully risk-informed strategic decisions with confidence. These experienced experts can also evaluate whether there is enough risk talent and technology deployed to fully empower the CEO and others to take informed risks in pursuit of your goals. What follows is a brief discussion of key elements these experts will look for — ones that, if not yet present, you can begin to consider for use.

Board committees

The governance of risk-taking — risk governance — is the purview and responsibility of the entire board of directors. Still, it is essential that some form of discussion and governance of risk takes place with more specific focus at the committee level. As you'll see in the next chapter, several dozen board members and C-level executives from around the world worked together and identified key board committees that can and should focus on risk in their charters and meeting agendas. To make for an easier transition at your organization, if needed, they've crafted several "guiding principles" documents that are practical and full of additional resources.

A committee that likely already exists at your organization and that should be including risk governance in their charter is the Compensation (Remuneration) Committee. Incentives often drive behavior, and well-intentioned articulations of corporate integrity and culture may be overwhelmed by unintentional creations of culture through pay systems. Further, as mentioned earlier in the book, the information available to your firm and your competitors about human capital via LinkedIn and other service providers has caused human capital risk to rapidly ascend in the rank of board priorities.

Your Audit Committee also may have risk governance in its charter. In general, the role of that committee tends to be backward-looking — seeking validation — when risk governance is primarily forward-looking — fostering anticipation. Risk governance is not entirely incompatible with the work of the Audit Committee, but it is viewed as a best practice to have a separate Risk Committee. So, you'll find a strong recommendation from me that boards include a Risk Committee as a stand-alone entity that takes any risk governance items off the current Audit Committee's agenda. With a growing presence of Risk Committees across various industries, their establishment and use are becoming fiduciary expectations.

Not all companies have a Technology Committee or its equivalent. However, the growing nature of Cyber Risk and Technology Risk usually warrants such at an organization of any complexity. This need especially applies to companies with geographically wide delivery of products and services or ones that use external contractors or critical digital suppliers, such as cloud services or software for pricing, risk, customer service, human resources, and more.

The effectiveness, empowerment, and focus of these three committees at your organization can be measured in comparison to the guidelines we'll highlight in the next chapter. And it should be noted that when the board makes a statement that risk governance is important enough to make these changes, it will signal an embrace of risk knowledge and improve the culture of the organization and its employees.

Corporate risk committees

Two senior management committees are most important for success in risk management — one which is standing and one which convenes only as necessary. The first is typically called a Risk Committee, but should not be confused with the one at the board level. You may consider naming it your Risk Management Committee to avoid this confusion. This committee usually will include senior business leaders, senior finance leaders, senior leaders from the risk management group, and may also engage senior operations leaders. Their job is to consider the ongoing and changing dynamic of the business environment in which the organization operates, the cost of acquiring capital to pursue corporate goals, the allocation of those costs to business units and specific projects, the risk-taking culture, and all aspects of living within the board-mandated limits on the pursuit of corporate objectives. The leader of this committee should have an indirect or direct reporting line to the board's Risk Committee or to the entire board.

The second committee is one that I mentioned earlier, which may be called a Problem Response Team. You'll also see it called an Emerging Risk Committee, or some other title that conveys its role to intercept and address emerging issues before they reach their full potential to cause damage. I served on one of these committees at U.S. Bancorp Piper Jaffray and was a firsthand witness to its effectiveness. To be successful, this committee needs full empowerment by the board and management committee, and cannot be second-guessed in hindsight. Put only those people on the team whom you trust totally. Best practice would be to include your most senior risk management officers, the heads of any business units being impacted by the emerging risk, your chief financial officer, and your general counsel. Any line or operations personnel that need to be called in will also participate, but to be effective the group must be small, senior, and decisive.

The Chief Risk Officer

But who is your most senior risk leader? In the early 1990s, I attended a conference on risk management in Boston. Far away from the main stage, up a few flights of stairs, and tucked away in a small room was James Lam, who was presenting to us his vision for something that back then was called "firmwide risk management." This term preceded the current standard expression — enterprise risk management. About 20 of us were in that room, so let's just say it was not the featured event of the conference.

James is commonly known as the world's first Chief Risk Officer, a title he garnered around the time of that conference. The title Chief Risk Officer was still uncommon as recently as 2007 — just before we entered the subprime crisis. I would estimate that fewer than 500 people held that title back then, while a search today on LinkedIn for Chief Risk Officer returns over 20,000 results. We've come a long way.

So, what is a Chief Risk Officer, and should you have one if you don't already? In short, the answer to the second question is "yes." A Chief Risk Officer, like any of your other C-level officers, has management committee responsibility for the overall risk management function at your firm. They may have just a few people directly reporting to them or several hundred under their leadership, depending on the complexity of the risks your organization has assumed, or plans to assume.

In organizations with simple risks or with budgets that preclude the dedication of a full-time employee to this role, you may consider the use of internal and external educational resources to raise the risk intelligence of your existing staff. Still, you'll want to assign the responsibility for aggregating your data and analysis around risk as part of an existing position's job description, making them a de facto Chief Risk Officer.

The Chief Risk Officer will typically report to the Chief Executive Officer, while also having indirect, unfettered reporting to the entire board, the Chair of the Board, or the chair of the board's Risk Committee. If you don't have a Chief Risk Officer now, at some point in the future you will wish that you did. I can assure you that the cost of an effective risk management infrastructure is dwarfed by the savings on the cost of capital that such a person's leadership will create.

As I mentioned, James Lam was the first Chief Risk Officer. He and I have become friends and have kept in contact since that conference, in part because we have had similar ideas on how organizations can best utilize risk in their pursuits. Fast-forward almost 30 years and James is now lauded as one of the global leaders in risk governance, and he chairs the Risk Oversight Committee of E*Trade, a publicly traded company that Morgan Stanley recently offered to acquire for $13 billion, or $58.74 per share.[1] At the time James joined the board, E*Trade stock was trading around $8 per share. It significantly outperformed the broad market between then and the time when the bid to acquire was received. James also has been named one of the top 100 directors in the U.S. by the National Association of Corporate Directors. He's done amazing work that has benefited many companies. This includes the very successful mortgage company I mentioned earlier in the book, as I took much of what I learned from James that day and put it to good use.

Risk Silos

Since good risk management requires transparency and timely communication, we want to know that risk is being examined and talked about at many different places and in many ways

---

1 *Morgan Stanley to buy E-Trade for $13 billion in latest deal for online brokerage industry*, Maggie Fitzgerald, CNBC, February 20, 2020.

across the organization. In short, we don't want *Risk Silos*. As the name implies, these are places where various forms of risk are separated from the others. This is less of a problem today, especially given the broader use of Chief Risk Officers, but it does still exist and can become problematic when one part of the firm is unaware of the risks being taken by another. That same vulnerability can stem from the interplay of various risk typologies within a single business unit or smaller group. Sometimes what appear to be diversified business units or initiatives have similar first principles of success and are thus highly correlated. Risk silos make these hidden elements more difficult to uncover.

In your hunt for risk silos, look for any place where the managers of risk are territorial or do not have proper escalation channels established — something we discuss next — or where risk typologies are not integrated to an enterprise-wide framework. When those are present, you need to take action to change the culture.

Escalation channels and policies

Ray Dalio, head of Bridgewater Associates, preaches and practices at his firm something he calls "radical transparency." In general, this means that any idea, any person, any item up for discussion should be examined in full and challenged in any way, with the ultimate goal being that everything they do gets better. In short, radical transparency is supposed to build trust, even if receiving critiques of your ideas might not feel good.

Radical transparency is about making sure the right people have the right information in time to make effective use of it. While there are some critics of Bridgewater's specific culture, within your organization you should still establish safe ways for any employee to rapidly escalate a concern to the Chief Risk Officer, to the CEO, or even to the board, in order to ensure critical transparency. These can include anonymous tip lines or regular and frequent off-the-record conversations between risk managers and those who are taking risk. Again, trusting that these escalations will not be met with retaliation, or any form of punishment, is essential for them to be successful. If you don't have this trust — or worse, if you don't even have these avenues deeply ingrained in your corporate culture — you cannot be resilient, and your ultimate cost of capital will be higher.

Trust-building: are your risk managers seen as value creators?

As an ideal and an aspiration, an organization that is making the best use of its risk-taking capacity — its risk capital — will have risk managers who are seen by the risk takers as contributing to the success of the organization.

For a time, mostly in the 1990s, it was in vogue to have risk managers as "cops" who would report people taking unnecessary risks. That was a destructive approach, and if it is in place at your firm, it should be exorcised. Instead, your independent reassurance functions should fulfill this role. Ensure that validation of controls and reporting is being kept in the realm of departments like Internal Audit and is not damaging the effectiveness of your risk managers. Risk managers and internal auditors can still have effective relationships to support the audit function. But if you find that your risk takers fear the risk managers, you'll lose nearly all the advantage of the risk governance model discussed in this book.

For this approach to be successful, risk managers must also trust that they will not be blamed for losses or negative risks being realized. They must be taught to think like businesspeople — to not fear risk as loss, especially of their career.

Education

Since all our organizations operate in dynamic environments, we must always be learning. For risk managers to be viewed as adding value to the organization requires ongoing education that has a two-way flow. First, risk managers need to be able to educate risk-takers and business line executives about how risk is priced, what they can do to lower their cost of risk, how their models and processes work, and generally to be a part of their ongoing discussions of good risks to take and how to achieve better returns if they are comfortable with their current levels of risk.

At the same time, business leaders and other risk-takers need to help the risk managers to understand the challenges and opportunities of their risk-taking activities. By doing this, the risk managers will develop an appreciation for challenges stemming from the constant onslaught of competition and of choosing which "dark rooms" to enter. Their models will get better, and their communication and understanding of the business most certainly will improve.

An evaluation of the quality and frequency of this two-way exchange will tell you much about the culture of your organization and whether the risk-takers are going to make the most effective use of the scarce commodity called risk capital.

An ethical culture

OCEG is an organization founded in the wake of the "dot-com crisis" when stock prices of tech companies rapidly deflated because investor expectations were not met. It was originally called the Open Compliance and Ethics Group, but now is simply referred to by its acronym.

OCEG is focused on something they call *Principled Performance*.[2] They define that as being comprised of, among other things, a principled purpose — your highest purpose as defined by the board — guiding your vision, values, and the organization's day-to-day activities, principled leadership, and a workforce comprised of principled people committed to the

---

2 Visit the OCEG website at *www.oceg.org/about/what-is-principled-performance* to learn more.

organization's purpose.

OCEG provides tools for the evaluation and development of this ethical culture in belief that it will be value-creating and thus part of the necessary infrastructure of any organization. Compliance with ethical norms is a minimum requirement for the establishment of broad trust between your organization and the providers of capital to it. So, the work of OCEG and the ethics and compliance workers in your organization is critical and should be both supported and validated by the board.

Agility

Leo Tilman and General Charles Jacoby have written an immersive text that defines a corporate culture of both strategic and tactical agility. Unlike the buzzword usage of this term, their book, *Agility*, examines how corporations create a consistent, repeatable ability to detect and assess changes in the competitive environment in real-time, and then take decisive action. All of this is done with a "will to win" enhanced by risk intelligence. Using their model, you can assess whether your organization's risk infrastructure has embraced true tactical agility.

This, and all that we have discussed in this chapter, should give you a better sense of what to look for and validate in the risk management infrastructure of your organization. We will next explore the best practices for your role in risk governance — something which takes place at the board level.

CHAPTER 7

Board Processes Around Risk and Risk-Taking

We've just looked at some of the key elements of good risk management by your organization's employees — things that you and your board should validate as existing and functioning well, or that you should have others outside of your organization validate for you. But there remains the fiduciary responsibility at the board level for risk governance and how you empower the taking and management of risk in pursuit of your strategic goals. This takes a different set of approaches, which we now will discuss.

Back in 2008, a group of board directors and C-level officers, including many Chief Risk Officers, began to share their best practices and risk intelligence with each other. The perspectives they brought together came from diverse industries and geographies. They were shared via in-person roundtables, online presentations and meetings, and through the dissemination of raw observations in what became known as the Crisis Sentiment Index — a gauge of the progression of economic and financial conditions around the world during the Great Recession.

This group, known as the Directors and Chief Risk Officers group, or the DCRO, eventually grew to more than 2,000 members from over 120 countries. Its work transitioned to the establishment of guiding principles around risk governance that were practical and specific, enabling boards around the world to begin to adopt best practices more easily. We examine those guiding principles documents here.

The Board Risk Committee

In November 2018, the DCRO published its Guiding Principles for Board Risk Committees. As mentioned in the last chapter, the existence of this committee at the board level is becoming a fiduciary expectation. As we see firms try to navigate the emerging pandemic in 2020 and its unique challenges, organizations that have established these committees are already faring better. And there is no doubt that more companies will be adding these committees to their board governance processes as we recover.

The background for this set of guiding principles points to something important for all boards and individual board members to recognize:

> Most board members are quite adept at and familiar with risk-taking. But experience in taking risk and understanding risk are not equivalent. Board-level risk governance is a process that involves dynamic analysis of an uncertain future, development of internal resilience, allocation of risk-taking capacity, establishment of measurable levels of tolerance for loss, and envisioning things that may never have been considered relevant to a business discussion, but which might have highly disruptive potential. This type of analysis is the realm of directors with a special understanding of risk and is the genesis of board risk committee inclusion in best practice corporate governance.

As noted, the purpose of this book is to help you establish an environment at your organization in which the most value can be created from its risk-taking capacity. The DCRO Guiding Principles for Board Risk Committees distinguishes the Risk Committee's role from others in the following ways:

1. Consistent with the idea that risk governance and risk-taking are about enhancing the future value of our organizations:

- Having the directive to look forward, not backward in time
2. Consistent with understanding the first principles of fulfilling your organization's purpose:
    - Developing a deep understanding of the drivers of success in achieving corporate goals
    - Building an awareness of any threats to those drivers of success, as well as any opportunities for their enhancement
    - Overseeing the organization's tolerance for loss relative to its objectives and accountabilities
3. And, as we discussed in the previous chapter and continue here:
    - Ensuring that the organization has the necessary infrastructure, expertise, and capabilities to identify emerging changes in the risk landscape and to provide early warning of corporate performance that materially deviates from expectations
    - Ensuring that the organization's infrastructure, culture, policies, and procedures foster resilience
    - Ensuring that the components of enterprise risk management are in place and that the overall program is working effectively
    - Driving the corporate risk culture throughout the organization
    - Conveying to external stakeholders and potential partners that management and the board understand risk and its potential for positive and negative impact

That last bullet point is critical. When key providers of capital are external, we need a committee like this to help enhance trust and thereby lower the cost of the capital being provided to us.

The full DCRO document guides on purpose, form and function, the committee's role in corporate communications, and provides an extensive list of questions that the committee should be able to ask and answer on behalf of the entire board.

As with all the guiding principles documents referenced in this chapter, the entire Guiding Principles for Board Risk Committees can be found at *www.dcro.org*, as well as on the resource page dedicated to readers of this book. There are sample Risk Committee charters referenced in the guiding principles document and on the resource page, the link to which is provided at the end of this book.

Compensation Committees and risk

As noted earlier, Compensation Committees are an essential element of board risk governance. Many organizations have discovered, and it has been well-researched in psychological literature, that incentives to act in certain ways can easily overwhelm verbal guidance and directives defining acceptable forms of behavior.

Critical questions about risk-taking and compensation practices focus on whether short, medium or long-term performance should be most rewarded, whether fixed or variable pay is appropriate for specific functions within the organization, whether individual or corporate performance is most important, whether pay should be at risk in the event of future performance issues, and whether pay should be formulaic, discretionary, or some combination of both.

According to the DCRO Guiding Principles for Compensation Committees:

> Through thoughtful contemplation and discussion of these questions, a board will be better prepared to pursue the positive outcomes of risk-taking. However, to fulfill a board's Duty of Care around pay governance, it

must ensure that compensation philosophy includes an effective communication of the goals an organization is pursuing, validate that the organization is carrying out that pursuit within the boundaries the board has set, and, both ex ante and ex post, understand the potential downside to risks that have been taken. Realized pay must then incorporate the board's understanding and evaluation of all three of these components into a successful culture, and should not solely contemplate and reward financial objectives that have been reached or exceeded. The failure to consider potential negative risks when determining incentive pay means that the Duty of Care cannot be fulfilled.

That last statement is rather direct and definitive. Some might think it unfair to hold the board accountable for failing to consider how pay structures could change the shape of future values to be more negatively skewed. In combination with the board Risk Committee's work, though, incorporating the guidance for Compensation Committees found in the DCRO document should suffice in fulfilling this fiduciary expectation.

The DCRO Guiding Principles for Compensation Committees were written to provide organizations with essential guidance for the governance of risks associated with compensation philosophy and pay culture. It is noted that the work of this specific committee is among the most difficult of board duties. Even if the committee's focus is primarily on CEO compensation, its work will impact nearly every employee in the company. Hence, the guiding principles focus on governing the broad tactical implementation of compensation philosophy. The guidance is given in such a way that its implementation creates a positive skew to future value of the organization.

The full DCRO document provides dozens of helpful questions that the board and the Compensation Committee need to be able to ask and answer, along with a diagram outlining an annual information flow through this committee to help ensure dynamic best practices of pay governance. Many other helpful documents are referenced as well, and provide greater detail regarding this challenging arena. You'll likewise find many of those documents listed on the resource webpage for this book.

Cyber risk governance

In June 2018, the DCRO risk governance council focused on Cyber Risk and Technology Risk, via its Guiding Principles for Cyber Risk Governance. The august group that assembled these principles included some extraordinary talent from around the globe, some with very specific responsibilities and expertise in confronting cyber crime in the commercial, intelligence, and government arenas.

The purpose of this document was to give boards the ability to govern the cyber security programs at their organizations to ensure that they are effective, which includes being appropriately dynamic. As the document states, cyber security cannot be guaranteed, but a timely and appropriate reaction can. Consistent with the overall theme of positive value from resiliency, the guiding principles document notes that the ability to quickly identify and respond to a problem will determine the company's ultimate recovery. The guidance from this governance council is to make cybersecurity a senior management issue, not just a technical one.

Unlike other forms of risk governance, cyber risk governance is guided by the board in only a defensive manner. In other words, it is primarily focused on resiliency and limiting loss, although, a better understanding of what constitutes an organization's digital "Crown Jewels" will give boards more insight on some first principles of success in the organization's endeavors. The value of these assets is one determinant of the sufficiency of your risk capital or risk-taking capacity. As the guiding principles say, "theft, unauthorized access, or damage to these assets could represent an existential risk." That clearly raises cyber risk governance to a board-level responsibility.

Also discussed in the document is the concept that some risk managers refer to as the Three Lines of Defense model. Noting that cyber risk management is focused on the defensive side of activities, the three-lines model is of even more value here than for some other risk-taking activities. Those three lines include risk identification and assessment, risk management, and risk monitoring. So, while perhaps more valuable in managing cyber risk, the approach also builds a firm foundation for taking risk confidently in pursuit of positive outcomes generally. Validation of its effective implementation is part of your board's governance duty.

This document has been the most popular of all DCRO guiding principles publications, perhaps because cyber risk is an ongoing phenomenon, evolving in response to advancing defenses. Like all good governance documents, the Guiding Principles for Cyber Risk Governance provides a framework and process for boards and board committees to effectively govern — not just manage — the process of mitigating cyber exposures. It is designed to evolve as threats emerge, thus building corporate resilience.

Finding Qualified Risk Directors

While my intent with this book was to keep the risk jargon to a minimum, you certainly had to endure some in our discussion of risk typologies. But the exposure to this common language is not designed to make each director who reads this book a risk expert. In fact, there is a very specific mindset that comes into play at the board level that is forward-looking, and the approach of someone the DCRO defined as a Qualified Risk Director is a bit unique.

In my work with directors, I've typically seen what I would describe as linear, multi-linear, and stochastic thinking about the future. Linear thinking sees a path forward and marches down it with confidence. As mentioned before, confidence can lead to success, especially if it is risk-informed confidence. Multi-linear thinking acknowledges multiple possible outcomes that could result from the strategic plans and execution by the workers of the company. Both styles complement each other and, in combination, dominate board rooms. The third mindset, the stochastic thinker, refers to someone who tends to be uniquely comfortable with risk as a forward-looking concept, both positive and negative, with all kinds of shapes to the distribution of myriad possible future outcomes. Just as it is important to have a diversity of experiences and perspectives on the board to avoid groupthink and to be more creative, having at least one insider with a stochastic mindset can add tremendous value, especially around the topic of risk governance.

With this goal in mind, the DCRO's first guiding principles document was created as a foundation to all that followed. It described the kind of acumen, personal attributes, education, and experience likely to be found in what it defined as a Qualified Risk Director. The spirit of the document is in keeping with the concept of an Audit Committee Financial Expert, but focuses on identifying someone who has these characteristics most essential for the governance of risk. This person is likely to be better suited for communication with the firm's risk management infrastructure and with general education of other board members in the concepts of risk as a commodity, having cost, and its association with trust and the overall cost of attracting capital.

Many of the characteristics described in this document are common among board members. They would be distinguished by the breadth of their presence among certain directors. What is interesting to note is that not long after these guiding principles were published, governance rating agencies began to analyze whether boards had risk experts, and to adjust their scores accordingly. These were parallel efforts, although each seems to be cross-validating.

While in this chapter I've highlighted four documents that will be very helpful to you as you build the critical infrastructure and processes for the board to successfully govern risk-taking, you'll find standards like that of the ISO 31000 to be very helpful as well. They were, perhaps surprisingly, derived from a very popular regulatory document called the Joint Australia New Zealand Standard — Risk Management Principles and Guidelines. As you finish reading this chapter and integrate what you've read here with what you learned about the best practices for your corporate risk infrastructure, you'd do well to reference the ISO 31000 document too. It is succinct, broadly applicable, and can be quite useful in your governance efforts.

As mentioned before, links to additional helpful documents like ISO 31000 are provided on this book's resource page, as is a link to a companion book which includes all of the DCRO guiding principles documents in one publication.

CHAPTER 8

A Process of Continuous Innovation: Avoiding the "Fade"

In the next two chapters, we're going to examine two critical elements in the successful establishment of a corporate culture and infrastructure that yields positively skewed future results. In this chapter, we will build further on the critical "why" you need to establish the risk governance concepts we cover in this book, in combination with our first look at the complex networks in which we pursue our goals. Our focus on networks will expand, but for now we will look at them as they exist, and then explore how to best utilize them in the next chapter.

First off, for any organization to be successful, it needs one critical thing: others. We need other people to see our products and services as being value-generating for them in a manner sufficient to warrant the exchange of their precious capital for what our organization offers. We can have extensive networks of potential capital providers in the realms of human capital, financial capital, and more, but without these customers or donors electing to give us their monetary capital, we cannot fulfill our purpose.

The concept of "fade"

Under non-pandemic conditions, your organization is likely doing well, or well-enough. But that's not always going to be true. In fact, as you'll see in this section and the next, there is a life cycle of corporate performance that should concern you as a fiduciary, even if your organization is growing exponentially right now.

Bart Madden and his colleagues at Callard Madden & Associates began in the late 1960s to look at whether there was a life cycle of companies that could be identified, and ultimately understood — a form of Principal Component Analysis that applied very broadly to for-profit companies. Madden's research was quite successful and yielded a concept now known as corporate "fade." It's a clever term to describe the common tendency of firms to see a whittling away of their excess returns over the cost of capital as they mature. Ultimately, when fade persists, firms will reach a point where their returns are equal to or below their cost of capital, at which point they have begun to destroy value, rather than create it. Figure 8.1 below illustrates this concept graphically.

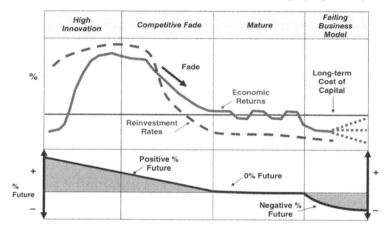

Figure 8.1: Corporate Fade. Source: Bartley J. Madden, *Value Creation Principles*, John Wiley & Sons, 2020 (used with permission).[1]

---

1 According to Madden, "We can estimate the value of a firm's existing assets from the present value of cash flows produced as the firm's existing assets wind-down. Deducting this estimated value of existing assets from the firm's known market value leaves the implied value of future investments. The % Future metric expresses the implied value of future investments as a percent of the firm's total market value. It answers the question: What does today's stock price say about the viability of a firm's likely future life-cycle performance?"

Fade reflects a lack of innovation. At the start of this book, I mentioned that the fear of taking risks is the surest way to realize failure, as our customers will ultimately leave us for better alternatives, or through simply finding little new value in what we do. Fade can be beaten through a process that Madden refers to as *knowledge-building proficiency*. His is a systems approach to understanding how organizations work, and has led him to the creation of something he calls The Pragmatic Theory of the Firm, highlighted in his contemporary book, *Value Creation Principles*.

Knowledge-building proficiency is a concept too rich for coverage in brief — although I'll give you more details later in this chapter — so I highly recommend that you read Madden's book. But in general, his conception is about tapping into the network of knowledge that we have, internally and externally, through the people involved in our firm's success. We'll come back to this general idea in the next chapter, as tapping into our networks is central to the governance model outlined in my book, *Governance Reimagined*. This means that both Madden and I think you should become very familiar with these ideas to do your best as a fiduciary.

In his book, Madden refers to the failure to have this knowledge-building proficiency as *firm risk:*

> Firm risk is about obstacles management faces that interfere with achieving the firm's purpose. Firm risk increases (decreases) in lockstep with changes that degrade (improve) the likelihood of achieving the firm's purpose. An increase in firm risk, all else equal, means a greater likelihood for a firm to generate lower future financial performance.

I tend to emphasize more the idea that failure is the negative side of risk, while implementing the improved risk governance structures covered in his book and mine will add positive risk that overwhelms or stunts the realization of negative risks from the failure to continuously innovate and create new value. But

I know from personal conversations that Madden is also very focused on the upside of risk-taking. He does make the very key observation that firm risk, in his definition, entails a long-term horizon. That mindset is critical, especially when paired with the resiliency-building structures and processes mentioned herein.

The initial research undertaken by Callard Madden & Associates was continued by a company called HOLT Value Associates, where Madden served as a partner. HOLT Value Associates was then acquired in 2002 by Credit Suisse. Madden reports in his book that as of today, many of the world's largest money management firms are clients of Credit Suisse HOLT and benefit from life-cycle valuation applied to more than 20,000 companies globally.[2] If you are a board member at a publicly traded company, this data is something with which you and your colleagues need to become familiar — if you are not already — as it appears to have been widely utilized by key financial capital providers who could be critical to your success.

The surprising mathematics of cities

If you've read *Governance Reimagined*, or Geoffrey West's bestselling book, *Scale*, you are familiar with both Dr. West and Complexity Science. The latter is one of the most important scientific innovations in our time, and it has applications to physics, finance, biology, sociology, economics, and more. If you are familiar with this concept, you have not been surprised by the spread and reaction to the outbreak of the novel Coronavirus. That's just one benefit of understanding Complexity Science.

West studies the relationships within complex systems. Complex systems are distinct from complicated systems in that the output (value) of the whole is significantly more than the sum of the parts. Your life, for example, is something that the parts of you could not do independently. You are more than the sum of your parts.

---

[2] Madden, Bartley J., *Value Creation Principles*, John Wiley & Sons, 2020.

Complex systems can be found in nature among plants and mammals, but companies and cities are also complex systems. They are the interacting and dynamic products of cooperation, competition, and knowledge-sharing. They often succeed with amazing results, and also can come crashing down in what is referred to as a complexity collapse. West notes that cities have shown the unique ability to survive incredible stresses, even nuclear bombs. Mammals, however, have demonstrated only temporary resiliency. As we all have been told, death and taxes are two of life's certainties.

So, West asks, are companies more like cities or mammals? Do they have the life cycle of a mammal: rapid growth, followed by leveling-off, and subsequent decay and death?

Sadly — and perhaps of no surprise to Madden, his colleagues, and the clients of Credit Suisse HOLT — companies look a lot like mammals. Independently and from a totally different perspective — that of a physicist — West found just what Madden and his colleagues had discovered. It is not encouraging, unless you begin to recognize why cities tend to live on and grow.

West points out that if companies want to escape the mammalian life cycle, they must innovate — an adaptation to the changing environment. Somewhat frighteningly, he says they must innovate at increasingly faster rates or they will lose this battle. While that sounds exhausting, it is, in fact, what cities do, what Madden gets at in his book, and what I write about in *Governance Reimagined*. It requires the engagement of those in our networks, high levels of trust, distribution of risk-taking authority, and more that you can learn a bit about in the next chapter, but which is covered extensively in *Governance Reimagined*.

Knowledge-building proficiency

But let's first take a closer look at knowledge-building proficiency.

According to Madden, the challenge facing most management teams is how best to improve the efficiency of existing assets, and sustain their organizations' competencies, while also investing in new opportunities. They must recognize and welcome that new opportunities may even have the potential to replace existing products or services. Again, see the story of Nokia that I referenced earlier in the book. In 2012, its board chair attempted to create a knowledge-building proficiency he called a culture of "paranoid optimism." This meant a culture of reality, combined with a form of radical transparency and a positive outlook for the future that was rooted in scenario-based thinking, was to drive its future.[3]

Madden describes knowledge-building as a dynamic process involving interactions with people of different experiences, part of what he calls a "knowledge-building loop." That loop includes a flow of ideas and information through our worldview — perceptions of us both internally and externally, the actions our organization takes, the risks it takes, and feedback from multiple sources. All of this then intersects with what we already know, and with our expressed — and, hopefully, adaptable — purpose for existing.

Again, a short treatment of Madden's concepts of knowledge-building proficiency and The Pragmatic Theory of the Firm is insufficient. But, like the museum I mentioned in the Introduction, I'm only giving you a quick glimpse of what's inside his book and telling you that you absolutely must visit it.

A portfolio mindset

This section of the chapter was originally titled "A Venture Capital Mindset," consistent with how I refer to it in *Governance Reimagined*. I was surprised to get some negative pushback from a board member for whom I have great respect. But her experience

---

3   See both. Madden, Bartley J., *Value Creation Principles*, John Wiley & Sons, 2020, and Siilasmaa, Risa, *Transforming Nokia: The Power of Paranoid Optimism to Lead through Colossal Change*. McGraw-Hill Education, 2019.

in this area had been more with what I refer to as Vulture Capitalists and their tendencies to take what they want from a company, leaving bare bones and unwanted flesh after they leave. So, let me explain the Portfolio Mindset and the ventures we must take to be more like cities that keep growing for millennia.

Diversification is a term used to describe risk-reduction in investment portfolios through the spread of investment capital across multiple, less-than-perfectly-correlated assets. Done properly, a portfolio of truly diversified assets will have a total investment risk that is below that of a portfolio which consists of just one similar-type asset, or even just a few. The future of that portfolio may be more likely to be positively skewed, and it is certainly in need of less capital to sustain it.

A venture capitalist is looking to create diversified portfolios of investments that are generally small at the start, at least individually. The goal is for them to nurture a relatively small percentage to large successes, and to ensure that those which fail do not harm their ability to continue the life of their whole portfolio. In other words, no bets are so big that they materially damage the overall venture fund. If you recall my reference to rampant incrementalism at the Principal Financial Group, you should see a parallel here.

Every organization is a portfolio of ideas, products, and services. It also is a portfolio of physical, human, and financial capital. Applying the concepts of portfolio — and yes, good venture portfolio management to our organizations — will greatly increase the likelihood that we sustain value creation, avoid downward competitive fade, and that we escape the mammalian life cycle by nurturing large gains, while limiting failed ventures. Because these large successes will also allow us to take more small bets, we can get to the point that West refers to, where our innovation is happening at a faster and faster rate.

In this successful venture world, three successes breed nine, which in turn breed 27, which then breed 81. And so on. Again, amidst the pandemic erupting as I write this book, that math may look familiar. It should, as pandemics also can spread at these rates and this is how the term "going viral" originated — something that, until 2020, was generally applied positively.

As you no doubt know, some start-ups do not have the luxury of diversification. In fact, some early-stage investors will decline to invest in start-ups that engage in this practice, wanting their entrepreneurial partners to be highly focused on the success of what they have created. That's just fine. This is still consistent with the venture capital mindset that drives the thinking I reference here.

Larger and more mature organizations are more likely to have boards of directors rather than venture capitalists that might lend management guidance to their portfolio companies. It is those entities that must put extra effort into ensuring their risk-taking culture continuously drives internal start-ups and innovation with a laser focus on the success of whatever they are trying. That approach is one of the keys to reaching a positive skew of future value.

In the next chapter, we're going to look at how to bring people into the knowledge-building loop — to help your organization with both innovation and resiliency-building. As governors of your precious assets, incorporating your networks and their knowledge will be essential for success.

CHAPTER 9

Ongoing Conversations and the Feedback Loop: Always Getting Better

We already have discussed elements of the corporate risk infrastructure that would be expected for your organization to have confidence in its ability to take risk well. One of those elements was someone with the title Chief Risk Officer. During the years since James Lam was first given that title, the role has evolved. In many places, it was put in place to alert management in advance so that "bad things didn't happen." In one lead risk management role that I had, albeit not with that title, the CEO told me he appreciated my contributions because they made him sleep better.

Progressing from these early days of risk leadership, you can now find Chief Risk Officers for various business units, or individual domestic units of multinational companies. In other words, some companies have multiple "chief" risk officers. In banking and some other industries, regulators now require the presence of a Chief Risk Officer and may even have the authority to approve the person in that role.

In 2007, I had a meeting with Dipak Jain, then the dean of Northwestern University's Kellogg School of Management — one of the most highly respected graduate business programs in the world. He was curious to learn more about the role of Chief Risk Officer. While I probably thought I would be changing his, and thus Kellogg's, view of the importance of that role, it was my view that was changed by Dean Jain.

In our meeting, he asked me how many Chief Risk Officers I

knew who had responsibility for the customer. Somewhat taken aback, I paused and answered, "none, that I know of." With a slight grin, he leaned back in his chair and wryly asked, "How can anyone be called a Chief Risk Officer when they don't have responsibility for the single biggest risk a company faces — not knowing their customers' needs in two years' time?"

From that day forward, I worked even harder to shift the mindset of others about their responsibilities as the heads of risk management. Through my experience at the mortgage company I mentioned earlier in this book, I already understood the link between good risk management and successfully meeting customer needs. But it was Dean Jain's essential distillation of company risk to that single element — your customers' future needs — that reprioritized my thinking on risk. Ours was a very valuable discussion, likely even more so for me than him.

Our organization's social network

That conversation with Dean Jain happened because I knew some people who were teaching at Kellogg at that time. I had met one of them when he was visiting the campus on which my wife served as a Pastor. I became acquainted with the other through my work leading an association of risk managers. These were connections that came about through other existing connections. Now, my connection to Dean Jain connects them all back to you. Why is this web of connections relevant?

We each recognize to some degree that we are part of social and professional networks. But most of us don't realize the hundreds of networks and systems with which we interact every day. I share one graphic in Figure 9.1 — a quite simple one, actually — that shows some of the people and companies involved in the life of Kevin Bacon, the actor best known for playing a character who danced when he wasn't supposed to. Kevin Bacon also is famous for being the subject of the game "Six Degrees of Separation from Kevin Bacon." In that game, you try to name people connected

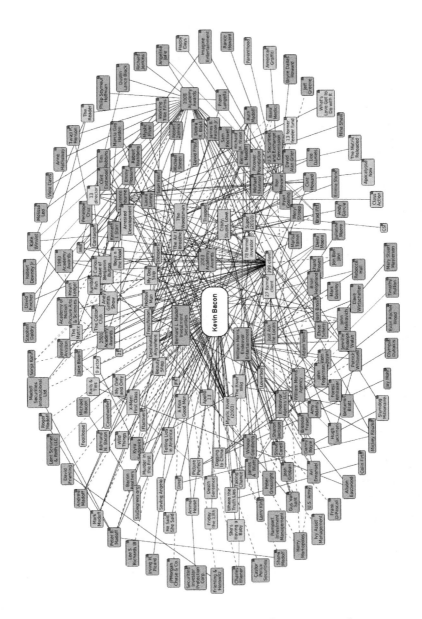

Figure 9.1: The Kevin Bacon Social Network. Source: *Muckety.com*

ONGOING CONVERSATIONS AND THE FEEDBACK LOOP

to each other that eventually connect to Kevin Bacon in less than six steps. "Six handshakes from the President" is another version of this game, which becomes no game during a viral pandemic.

His network looks complicated. In fact, it is quite complex, as we discussed before. Kevin could not be as successful as he has been without this network. And even if some of the people in it say bad things about him, his overall body of work has made him a star.

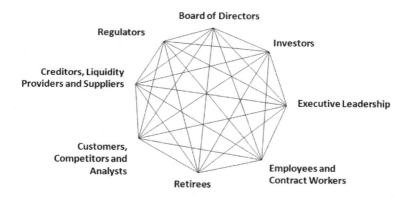

Figure 9.2: The forces of change on organizational value.

We focus here on the positive and important engagement of our organization's social network in our governance of risk-taking. Every organization has a network like the one depicted in Figure 9.1. People and other organizations engage with us as capital providers, customers, gossipers, competitors, neighbors, and more. In a very simplified format, the lines of communication about us can be represented as they are in Figure 9.2, where every entity named here has the ability to influence the future value of our organization, both positively and negatively.

This chapter is about how to use them most positively.

Engaging your social network

The governance model outlined in *Governance Reimagined* is called a networked and distributive governance model. I've hinted earlier that one of the outcomes of good board risk governance infrastructure and process is the ability to more confidently empower employees to take risk — seizing opportunities that create value even if some losses are incurred along the way. That's a big part of the distributive element, as is their ability to intercept emerging negative risks to help with our resiliency. Both build towards a positive skew of future value.

But boards of directors have been entrusted by multiple entities that make commitments to engage an organization, including investors, suppliers, regulators, lenders, customers, and employees. High-commitment relationships like these are essential for success. And every one of those groups can bring value to our process.

Bart Madden writes about utilizing feedback from these groups to sustain a knowledge-building culture, similar to the "networked" element of my preferred governance model. For the purposes of this guidebook, I am just going to highlight a few elements of the networked side of that model to help us bring in some of the best intelligence about our customers' future needs, as well as the capital we will need to fulfill them, through engagement of our organization's social network.

Stakeholder boards

Many directors have a visceral reaction to the use of the term "stakeholders." While leading investment companies like BlackRock, it's CEO and Chairman Larry Fink, and the Business Roundtable have begun to emphasize that all companies have a duty of care beyond that which is expected by owners in the short run. It is their argument that such is in the long-term interest of owners. And I agree.

Remember, risk-taking requires capital in all its forms. Capital is a commodity, which means risk needs to be talked about and treasured like a scarce commodity. Every stakeholder has the potential to increase or decrease the cost of that capital, which means they have the ability to increase or decrease the cost of taking risk. If the cost of taking risk goes up, the hurdles beyond which our portfolio of risk-taking and innovation activities must pass are higher, meaning we can take fewer risks. Fewer risks in the portfolio means that it is less diversified and more likely to have adverse outcomes in total, and less likely to realize high-flying successes.

So, we want to find a way to engage these stakeholders to learn from them and to give them a sense of ownership in our success as well. Other than our competitors, none of those in our organization's social network want us to fail.

One method to achieve this is to create stakeholder boards which can informally advise the board of directors on emerging concerns or needs. A more extreme model creates a board of stakeholders that is empowered to veto company plans — a far more radical idea than most are willing to consider, but one that would signify an immense level of trust and engagement. Or, the board can ensure that various stakeholder boards are being engaged by business leaders, or even front line risk-takers. That too is a positive form of risk governance.

Whatever the approach, the important part is that those on whom you rely for your success can give you active intelligence on how their views of you and your offerings are changing.

Executive sessions with employees

We can enhance this feedback through those who regularly interact with these stakeholders. While boards often meet with the CEO, CFO, Chief Risk Officer, or other management committee members, the story presented may sometimes be filtered, intentionally or unintentionally, to the desires or benefit of that elite group. This is one form of misinformation risk that was mentioned in Chapter 3.

By bringing in employees in various roles and from various parts of the organization to meet with the board's Risk Committee, a new, ideally validating, picture of the firm's prospects and performance can be attained by the board. These meetings are not intended to breed a sense of distrust of the management committee members. Rather, they are meant to give the board more confidence to empower the management committee, which furthers the distributive nature of good risk governance. It winds up creating more freedom for management, not less.

Asked to comment on how her organization was successfully managing the challenges of the COVID-19 pandemic, Dr. Penny Wheeler, President and CEO of the Allina Health System, recommended the following for leaders: "Learn as much as you can from the people who are the closest to the work. They will help to guide your choices and decisions and there is genius that exists out there that you need to listen to."[1]

Identification of Commons

Earlier I mentioned that all the members of our organization's social network, with the exception of our competitors, want us to succeed. It is in our common interest for that to happen. Common interest, though, is not to be confused with something called a Commons, although they are related.

You may have heard an expression, "the tragedy of the Commons." It was made famous by Garrett Hardin when he talked about how lack of government regulation of common-pool resources, or Commons, almost ensured their demise. Air, water, and grazing lands are examples of Commons that have been abused and nearly destroyed in many locations. In truth,

1 *CBS Sunday Morning*, interview with Ted Koppel, "What kind of leadership does our nation need?", April 12, 2020.

Commons don't need to be tragically abused. Nobel-winning research has shown how self-governance of Commons can actually lead to a far more efficient use of those resources than could any government regulations or any typical hierarchical management structure. It's a powerful model, and one that makes it important for us to identify Commons in our organization.

One of the most obvious and important Commons is our brand or reputation. Remember, our reputation is our ability to influence or persuade. The better our reputation, the greater influence we have. Greater influence means that it's easier to attract capital, and ... you know the rest. Our reputation also affects our perceived value. Among large publicly traded companies, the percentage of total market value that is "intangible" has grown from 17% in 1975 to 84% in 2015.[2] Intangible value, as its name suggests, is purely about the impression investors have of your company's ability to meet their expectations of the future. It reflects the market's trust in your ability to innovate along with the value of your brand or reputation. The latter is estimated to account for as much as 25% of the intangible value of large publicly traded companies.[3]

But it's not just publicly traded companies that have intangible value which can impact the ability to fulfill our purpose. Intangible value is seen even by nonprofits when some find it easier to attract donors than others also expressing a need for funding.

Another Commons is our total capacity to take risk. While not entirely separate from our brand or overall corporate reputation, management of that Commons is an activity that takes place once capital has been secured. In fact, there are multiple Commons of this type throughout our organization at every point where a new or existing initiative begins to use capital. We begin

---

2 Ocean Tomo, 2015 Intangible Asset Market Value Study.

3 Elston, Kate, and Hill, Nick, Intangible Asset Market Value Study, *les Nouvelles — the Journal of the Licensing Executives Society International*, Vol. LII No. 4, September 2017.

to see that the links between the cost and the benefit of risk-taking are most effectively managed once the capacity to take risk is seen as a common-pool resource that we do not want to be abused.

Successful Commons governance

The Nobel Prize winner I alluded to previously is Elinor Ostrom. She passed away in 2012, but her work on successful Commons governance is remarkable and she lives on through its influence on business and regulation.

In Ostrom's model, there are eight principles that must be applied and be present for the achievement of success. I paraphrase and modify them here, so that they apply to the governance and management of organizations, as opposed to water, air, or other natural Commons.

1. There must be clear boundaries established into which risk capital is allocated.

2. The objectives and rules that limit behaviors in pursuit of corporate goals must be understood.

3. Within the boundaries established in #1 above, members of the group with access to that group's risk capital have an unfettered freedom to re-allocate that capital subject to the rules and objectives established in #2 above.

4. All activities are monitored by people internal and external to the group, including stakeholders — high levels of transparency.

5. If there are abuses, they must be met with punishments that get larger as the infraction or frequency of infractions grows.

6. There must be an independent means to settle conflicts within each group.

7. So long as the rules are being followed, the freedom

granted to each group must be respected and not arbitrarily changed.

8. All of these groups are nested within some larger entity, in effect, creating a diverse portfolio of risk-taking activities.

Trust and positive amplification

You see the word "freedom" twice above. Freedom cannot be fully realized without trust. Trust comes through a process that gives the board confidence in the risk-taking activities of the firm. The more trust that is given and the more that trust is validated through the eight principles above, the more likely it is that your organization can begin to experience viral growth of the magnitude Geoffrey West said is needed to escape from the normal path of organizations towards death.

But this positive amplification doesn't come from just our internal portfolio of activities and ideas. By engagement of stakeholders in our process, they too will have a sense of ownership in what we do and can act as positive amplifiers of our corporate goals and desire to be more valuable to them all.

Higher trust means lower ... okay, enough. By now you should have this memorized. We're getting to the positive skew that is the ultimate goal of every board in the fiduciary role they have. Making that more likely is one of the most important ways that I hope this book, and the other resources to which I direct you, will bring benefit to your organization.

CHAPTER 10

The Next Steps to Take with Your Board Colleagues

Through nine chapters of this brief book, I've tried to give you a tour guide's introduction to ideas that can help you transform risk from something we fear into something we put to use in pursuit of our goals. Our organizations exist for a reason. They have been successful enough to warrant the creation of, and governance demands from, a board of directors. You are in your fiduciary role because you've been successful in your work too. But you will need to do more as demands change. And you, personally, have even more to contribute to our global or local well-being, whatever market your organization serves.

So, what do you do next to create value through the embrace of risk? What can you do to enhance the trust that others have in you and to build your resiliency?

In my work, I recommend that organizations take five steps to achieve such growth:

Step 1: Prioritize Trust — As I've tried to emphasize in this book and in my other writing, the foundation of all that you do is the establishment of high levels of trust among those interested in your success. The actions you take in this first step are about evaluating the levels of trust among internal governors (you and your fellow board members) and key innovators in your company. You quickly move to the same assessment of your relationship with external members of your organization's social network. Just ask them via one-on-one conversations or using more broad surveys of these key parties. Or, look for demonstrations of existing trust or places where you've seen key people turn away from you, and seek to understand better the first principles of those actions.

Capital providers crave trust. Companies like MSCI, Thomson-Reuters, Sustainalytics, and ISS all sell governance, environmental, and sustainability ratings on publicly traded companies. Charity Navigator and others rate the quality of nonprofits. Moody's, S&P Global, Fitch, Dun & Bradstreet, and Kamakura are among firms providing corporate credit risk assessments. These organizations would not exist if there weren't any demand for greater trust in our partners.

The next steps will help you to address any shortcomings you find from your self-assessment.

Step 2: Further Engage Your Internal and External Networks — Even if trust levels are already high, you and your fellow board members should begin to look for ways in which you can improve the engagement of key parties to your success. You can establish stakeholder boards, or at least ensure that the people who are closest to the risks you are taking have clear avenues of escalating emerging issues and demands from those we serve — and on whom we depend to support and supply us. You can use the survey data mentioned in Step 1, or read reports from governance ratings agencies and other analysts. These evaluations will give you a sense of how you are being portrayed relative to other entities that are competing for the same capital as you. As I've tried to emphasize, these key allies are harbingers of potentially positive and negative risks, and are essential to your growth and longevity. Understanding what they know and feel or believe can be highly valuable.

Step 3: Create the Conditions for Innovation — Innovation is essential for your continued growth. As Geoffrey West notes, to grow at a rate that ensures your long-term survival, you need to keep innovating at an increasingly faster pace. Innovation happens when there are strong levels of trust and engagement among the key parties to your success. And knowledge-building, along with a venture portfolio mindset to risk-taking, is essential as you work to establish the channels that allow experimentation, nurturing of success, and control of the downside risk of trying new things.

You also need your risk managers to be working closely with your risk-takers, providing them with insight on the line-item cost of risk. If this capability doesn't yet exist at your firm, now is the time to begin your investment in the necessary resources. I can promise you a return on investment unlike almost anything else you do.

Finally, you should examine your compensation plans and philosophy using the guiding principles developed by the DCRO. Ensuring that these strong signals of corporate intent are aligned with your goals, objectives, and intended culture is essential for your success.

Step 4: Leverage Your Discoveries — Completing, or even just beginning, the first three steps will lead you to both new ideas and new risks. The discovery of each gives you opportunity and a greater need for resiliency. This process brings new levels of understanding to both executives and board members, and may increase your needs for expert talent among employees and on the board.

As alluded to in Step 3, you may need to employ a Chief Risk Officer or create a risk management department. You might also need a Qualified Risk Director among your board colleagues.

The flow of information from the board to the organization and back needs to be continual, expert, and via multiple channels to ensure that your organization does not become subject to general groupthink or reactive to fear. If you take these proactive steps in response to your discoveries, you'll sleep better at night *and* take risk more confidently, which is our fifth step.

Step 5: Empower Your Risk-Takers — With this new knowledge comes greater confidence to take risk and to distribute the risk-taking to those in your organization who can do the most with it. The networked and distributive form of governance gives your organization the ability to best pursue your goals, while also giving you the trust needed to allow it to do so. This empowerment is about fostering early adaptation to a changing environment and early recognition of obsolete assumptions. To implement it, you have to change the way in which you conceive of, and talk about, risk and risk-taking towards a more positive framing.

Before you can fully implement Step 5, you must complete the first four steps. Part of the necessary information to do this relates back to potential losses from risk-taking. But that's not our lead when considering risk. Rather, the way in which your risk-takers are charged for risk will transform both your and their understanding of how the organization is exposed, and which projects, clients, and new businesses are worth pursuing.

Identifying key stakeholders

Through the process of Principal Component Analysis at the board level, you will discover several key parties to your success. These include high revenue customers, critical suppliers, mavens in your industries, retired executives and line employees, active line employees, regulators, liquidity providers, and any entity whose positive change in trust of your organizations will materially reduce your cost of capital and increase your ability to persuade.

Throughout the five steps outlined above, names will emerge, especially from line employees, that you at the board may never have considered as keystones to your success. Keep building and updating this list as time moves forward and your needs change. Let these people know that they are a valued part of your success.

Addressing Environmental, Social, and Governance concerns

Much like the reaction to the term "stakeholder" that I described earlier, when some people hear about environmental stewardship, social responsibility, or governance best practices — commonly referred to as ESG, they cringe and assume it's another way in which outside parties want to restrict businesses from pursuing profit. In fact, the data shows this to be the opposite of reality. Back in 2009, when I first met with investment managers about the value of corporate governance in the improvement of investment portfolio performance, skepticism abounded. Granted, we were coming out of the worst financial market conditions that most of them had ever experienced, and risk-taking on new ideas was viewed as potentially career-ending. But the notion that "governance" was a risk factor which could be used in portfolio construction was quite foreign.

Since those days, according to the Global Sustainable Investment Alliance, the amount of money in funds that invest based on sustainability criteria has grown from a negligible sum to over $30 trillion.[1] And some estimates are that an additional $20 trillion is set to flow into this form of investing over the next two decades.[2] As I mentioned in the last chapter, BlackRock CEO and Chairman Larry Fink is leading his firm's $7.4 trillion in assets towards an emphasis on greater responsibility from corporations to their broad communities.[3] Even if you don't plan to tap into the public capital markets to raise money in support of your activities, this movement should clearly demonstrate a change in the business environment and expectations from all capital providers. If you are not governing your risk-taking well, it will cost you — maybe more than your competitors.

To perhaps take a bit of the edge off any negative reaction to ESG, begin to view it as a subset of governance — your work

---

1   *2018 Global Sustainable Investment Review*, Global Sustainable Investment Alliance.
2   Stevens, Pippa, *Your complete guide to investing with a conscience, a $30 trillion market just getting started*, CNBC, December 19, 2019.
3   Estimated assets under management as of December 31, 2019. Source: *www.blackrock.com: About BlackRock: Who We Are*, last accessed March 31, 2020.

— and not vice versa. The "G" in ESG tends to focus on standard tick-the-box factors like board chair–CEO separation and like-minded metrics. Governance, on the other hand, is how a company lives, how it pursues its objectives, and what it expresses as its values — not just in writing, but also by its actions and the environment it establishes. This should include a focus on ESG factors and their impact on your perceived value.

Gap identification

You know that you have had a successful career, and others have validated that too. Look around your boardroom. Everyone there has some level of success in what they have done or currently do. But essential to the trust among board members is humility, respect, and a recognition that as your portfolio of risk-taking changes, so too will the demands of your strategic thinkers.

In my work, I have acted as a mediator between activist owners and the boards of their target companies, helping each to understand the merits of the other's positions. In one such case, the owners of a company had surprising barriers to their ability to appoint board members. This restriction was one source of problems in the relationship between the owners and the board. The goal of my work with them was to enhance their relationship — to build trust. In the process, it became clear that the company also needed to better understand the current gaps in their board talent.

This, as you can imagine, made the engagement a more difficult tightrope to walk. Businesses in this company's industry faced high regulation, rapidly encroaching competition, rapid technological changes, underfunded pension liabilities, heavy fixed infrastructure investments, and rapidly changing customer demands. Further, due to competitive pressures and regulations, the market gave companies in their industry very little control over the prices they could charge for their products and services.

Despite the commitment of every board member to its

success, a survey of the strategic needs required to successfully navigate that massive conflagration of competitive challenges — any one of which has knocked other businesses to the point of value destruction and failure — showed there was not one single board member who had dealt with even half of those issues in their professional career. Some board members had never dealt with any such concerns while in a leadership role. The owners recognized this shortcoming and its potential long-term costs. But the board, collectively, did not.

While through this mediation we were able to improve the relationship between the owners and their board, when it came time to consider real change, the board members involved in this process circled the wagons and used what political capital they had to ensure their continued control of the board. Perhaps it was fear of the board's experience gaps being pointed out that triggered the fight, not flight, response. Regardless, the organization almost surely will suffer in the coming years because of that pushback. They don't see the Gray Rhinos charging at them — they just don't have the right experiences to notice them.

It is essential that you have an honest and open discussion with your board peers about the gaps that exist which affect your ability to take risk confidently. This doesn't mean that you must ask board members to depart, although in some cases it might. Through your Nominating Committee, you can consider expanding your board or committing yourself to greater advancement in your own understanding of risk governance. As you replace retiring members, seek out those who fill these missing needs.

Learn from others who planned to be resilient

Most of our organizations are experiencing contemporaneous disruptions to our normal routines during the response and adjustment to the COVID-19 pandemic. There have been many examples of companies that clearly had not fully considered how to continue to keep their stakeholders' trust: firing employees who complain about possible exposure, telling suppliers who are owed money that they will not be paid, and more actions that signal an inward-looking, fear-driven, survival response.

But we also have learned of companies like H-E-B, the beloved Texas-based grocer, in a story documented by two writers for *Texas Monthly*.[4] According to the article, in early March 2020, H-E-B extended sick leave for workers and quickly instituted social distancing measures at each of their stores. They adjusted store hours to keep up with the needs of their stockers, and provided an escalation hotline specifically related to issues about the novel Coronavirus. And in mid-March, they also raised worker pay by $2 per hour.

Since 2005, the organization had been working on a pandemic and influenza response plan as part of their overall problem response planning. Said H-E-B President Craig Boyan, "We take being a strong emergency responder in Texas, to take care of Texas communities, very seriously." That's a clear and direct statement that builds trust with stakeholders, and that's why you hear people raving about the company.

H-E-B had a pandemic plan. By early February 2020 they had turned it into a tabletop exercise like the one discussed in Chapter 4. Subsequently, they maintained close contact with suppliers and looked to retailers in China, Italy, and Spain to learn about their experiences. They reported extensive cooperation from these partners.

It's still early in the pandemic, and we're just seeing the beginnings of the knock-on economic effects and human toll, so we don't know if H-E-B's plans will sustain their success. But we do know they have done a wonderful job earning even more trust from their stakeholders, who are facing a challenge few of them anticipated in the way that H-E-B's emergency preparedness team did.

---

4 Solomon, Dan and Forbes, Paula, "Inside the Story of How H-E-B Planned for the Pandemic," *Texas Monthly*, March 26, 2020.

Said Boyan, "We describe ourselves as a purpose-driven company, and we're at our best amid times of crisis." Understanding your purpose and the drivers of your success are key, and you can learn from the examples of others.

In a 2019 study by consultancy EY, only 21% of board members felt "very prepared" to respond to an adverse risk event. It is unlikely that when answering that question in 2019 any taking the survey were considering a global pandemic and its broad impact. In contrast, in an April 2020 survey, members of the DCRO said that almost 70% of their companies were satisfied with the effectiveness of their organization's resiliency planning even in the midst of the pandemic. Further, 74% said they were already discussing how to improve their plans. These data points suggest an active knowledge-building loop is in place at these firms. Neither result should be surprising, as membership in the DCRO is dominated by board members, chief risk officers, and C-level executives from firms that have demonstrated they place a high value on risk governance.

And, in one last example, we have to highlight the impact of the Internet on general economic resiliency. The Internet was designed to ensure communication during extreme events like a nuclear war. In this pandemic, that resource has allowed researchers to communicate and share data in ways that inevitably will lead to faster, more innovative, and perhaps more effective approaches to dealing with the crisis.

Internet communication has also moderated the economic impact of the pandemic on those who have access to technology and has hastened the education of the public on what to do to minimize the spread of the virus. The resiliency of that network has allowed many to continue their professional work, albeit at an altered rate. That resiliency has created value.

Engage exemplary board members

In recent years, the Directors and Chief Risk Officers' group has honored a small group of board members, naming them as DCRO Exemplars. At present, there are fewer than 20 to have received this honor and you can find their names and links to their biographies at *www.dcro.org*. The qualities a DCRO Exemplar should possess are integrity, innovation, leadership, and service — things we may also seek from our own organization collectively, and certainly from our leaders. (See more details on these qualities in the box below.)

These are also attributes that you have seen mentioned or inferred throughout this book. People or organizations with these

---

Qualities of a DCRO Exemplar

Integrity — Someone who demonstrates, articulates, and expects the highest ethical standards. Someone who is recognized by the markets, or in other public media, for their high professional standards. And, someone who demonstrates the importance of understanding and governing risk at an advanced level.

Innovation — Someone who has demonstrated work to advance the use and governance of risk in pursuit of corporate goals and has been recognized for contributions to innovations in risk governance. These people have taken unique and effective approaches to improved risk governance in their work.

Leadership — Someone who exhibits and maintains courage and leadership, doing what is best for those who depend upon them for success. Someone with demonstrated trust from their peers, markets, or other public media and who shows individual excellence demonstrated beyond what is typical for their industry or field.

Service — Someone who shows a devotion of time and resources to the continual improvement of risk governance within their organization and to the continual improvement of risk governance outside of their own organization via professional associations or other avenues.

traits help to create a positive skew to your future value and your ability to realize your goals.

You probably know many directors like those identified by the DCRO, and I would encourage you to reach out to them and share best practices in any way that you can. Organizations like the NACD (National Association of Corporate Directors) also identify exemplars with their own criteria. In short, let's all aspire to be seen in such a light with our actions, which include collaboration to the fullest extent permissible.

Embrace diversity of opinion

Over and over again I speak about the value of trust. Risk-taking is about that which will enhance the trust of all capital providers in your organization. I've also mentioned the need for board members to have humility and respect for each other, and to seek out opinions different from their default mindset.

This means that diversity of experience, gender, culture, industry, educational focus, etc. are key to your success as a board. But even more important is creating the environment in which every board member has a safe harbor in the boardroom — a place to flourish. This doesn't mean that you cannot challenge each other in the discussion. But those challenges need to be undertaken with respect and the open-mindedness of a new learner.

One of the things I enjoy most about writing books and articles is the research that I do in the process. The world is full of amazing thinkers who bring new perspectives to me on widely ranging subjects. I've become better at my work because of these people.

Bring humility and recognize our broad opportunity

I've also become better at my work because of my many failures and mistakes, which fortunately have been part of a portfolio of efforts that, overall, is still active and growing.

In life, I've also gained humility and appreciation through family tragedies and material health issues. Many of us have had similar experiences and, as I write this book, a massive effort is underway to avoid broad-scale tragedy and the ensuing familiarity with loss that it appears so many will garner. And while the resiliency of the Internet has contributed positively to our management of the crisis, it also has made us far more aware of the unequal distribution of the pandemic's economic and health impacts across varying income levels and demographic groups, highlighting an addressable social need to which you may choose to apply your talents.

We are mortals, and the duration of our time as contributing members of human life is uncertain. We do our best to share the lessons we've learned with our children, our colleagues, and others whom we encounter on our path.

Each of us will experience both success and failure in these efforts, but by guiding our efforts in the boardroom with a positive embrace of risk-taking in pursuit of the betterment of our organizations, we will not fail. Our organizations are complex systems whose parts will change over time, in successful ways, as long as we establish and nurture the conditions for that to happen.

That's our board's opportunity and our primary fiduciary duty.

What's next?

First, I hope that this book will generate new conversations about positive risk-taking among you and your board colleagues.

Second, I hope that you will share this book with others.

Third, I hope that you will make use of the online resources available to you that are directly relevant to the topics covered in this book. These resources, along with a variety of additional information, are available at *www.davidrkoenig.com/boardrisk*.

Last, I hope that you will share your feedback with me on this book and the ideas herein. As I mentioned before, I love to learn from others and know that there is still much to consider in terms of improving how we all work together to achieve whatever mission it is that we serve.

Please enjoy your journey.

APPENDIX

The Meaning and Importance of a Positive Skew

In this book I often reference the term *positive skew*. If it's not a familiar concept to you, I hope this appendix is helpful. I'll try to tell the story of its importance with some pictures.

When risk managers, or statisticians, try to describe something unknown, but which they would like to measure, they often use what is called a probability distribution to come up with their best guess. For example, if you'd like to know how much the stock market might go up next year, you could look at all of the data you have on its performance in past years and venture a guess as to what might happen next. You might also have some sense for the range of possible returns — how wrong your estimate might be. I'm not recommending this approach, just using it as an example.

Below is the well-known "bell curve" distribution. It shows the expected future value in the middle and an equal number of possibilities above and below that value.

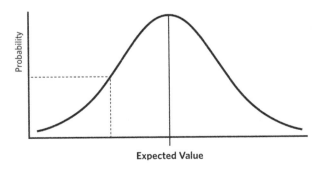

The left side is a mirror of the right side. And if you draw a line from any value below the expected value on the bottom axis and continue that line over to the left axis, the value on that axis tells you the chance that the actual future value will be below that value. When the distribution used is an accurate reflection of the future, this kind of an approach can be helpful in determining credit ratings or figuring how much capital you need to have to support your business. You might also use it as a measure of how much risk capital you need for a new product, investment, or project. But please note, almost no distributions of future value look like a bell curve!

The next two charts show distributions with negative and positive skews. Notice the difference in their shapes?

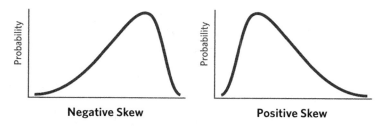

Negative Skew   **Positive Skew**

The positively skewed distribution climbs steeply on the left. It doesn't go very far to the left of center, and it stretches much farther to the right. If this is an accurate description of possible future values, there is a much higher chance of seeing a very large increase in value in the future and a much smaller chance of seeing a large loss. You can get this shape for your organization by fostering the kind of innovation we talked about in the book, combined with the things mentioned that help to interrupt problems before they reach their full potential to destroy value — your resilience.

Another interesting thing about the positively skewed distribution is that in this illustration the median value is the same as the bell curve. Half of the values are above and half are below, but because of the larger possible gains and smaller possible losses, the expected future value is higher than the bell curve distribution and much higher than the negatively skewed distribution. That means your organization is worth more! Your efforts are more likely to create value than to destroy it.

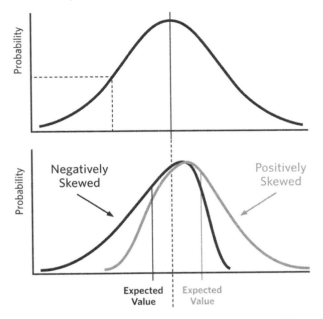

Everything we've talked about in this book has been focused on trying to get your organization to have a distribution of future values that looks positively skewed. We want you to be worth more, so that you can better fulfill your mission, whatever that might be.

If you take the steps to do this, your organization will continue to attract all forms of capital — physical, human, financial, etc. — more easily than organizations that are just "normal." And you'll be much more successful than companies that take risk without the kind of knowledge you will have. Those firms have a negative skew to their future.

We want to be positively skewed!

APPENDIX

Made in the USA
Middletown, DE
18 August 2023

36937580R00066